Chocolate

Publications International, Ltd.

Louis Weber, CEO
Publications International, Ltd.
8140 Lehigh Ave
Morton Grove, IL 60053

Pictured on the front cover: Chocolate Storm *(page 112).*

Pictured on the back cover *(clockwise from top):* Chocolate Espresso Cake *(page 120),* Double Chocolate Cookies and Cream Mousse *(page 154)* and Chocolate Chip Brownie *(page 63).*

ISBN: 978-1-63938-606-2

Manufactured in China.

8 7 6 5 4 3 2 1

Microwave Cooking: Microwave ovens vary in wattage. Use the cooking times as guidelines and check for doneness before adding more time.

WARNING: Food preparation, baking and cooking involve inherent dangers: misuse of electric products, sharp electric tools, boiling water, hot stoves, allergic reactions, foodborne illnesses and the like, pose numerous potential risks. Publications International, Ltd. (PIL) assumes no responsibility or liability for any damages you may experience as a result of following recipes, instructions, tips or advice in this publication.

While we hope this publication helps you find new ways to eat delicious foods, you may not always achieve the results desired due to variations in ingredients, cooking temperatures, typos, errors, omissions or individual cooking abilities.

Let's get social!
@Publications_International
@PublicationsInternational
www.pilbooks.com

Contents

Chocolate for Breakfast

Chocolate Hazelnut Biscuit Roll-Ups

MAKES 12 SERVINGS

- **2¼ cups all-purpose flour**
- **¼ cup granulated sugar**
- **1 tablespoon baking powder**
- **½ teaspoon baking soda**
- **½ teaspoon salt**
- **½ cup (1 stick) butter, cut into pieces**
- **¾ cup buttermilk**
- **1 teaspoon vanilla**
- **1 cup chocolate hazelnut spread**
- **½ cup chopped hazelnuts, toasted* (optional)**

****To toast hazelnuts, spread on baking sheet. Bake at 350°F 6 to 8 minutes or until lightly browned, stirring frequently.***

1. Preheat oven to 350°F. Spray 12 standard (2½-inch) muffin cups with nonstick cooking spray.
2. Combine flour, granulated sugar, baking powder, baking soda and salt in medium bowl; mix well. Cut in butter with pastry blender or two knives until mixture resembles coarse crumbs. Stir in buttermilk and vanilla just until blended. Turn out dough onto lightly floured surface; knead briefly to form a ball.
3. Roll out dough into 12-inch square. Spread chocolate hazelnut spread over dough to within ½ inch of edges; sprinkle with hazelnuts, if desired. Roll up tightly jelly-roll style; pinch seam to seal. Roll log back and forth to even out dough. Cut crosswise into 12 slices; place slices cut sides up in prepared muffin cups.
4. Bake 15 minutes or until golden brown. Immediately remove to wire rack; cool slightly.

Chocolate Doughnuts

MAKES 14 TO 16 DOUGHNUTS

- 2¼ cups all-purpose flour
- ½ cup unsweetened cocoa powder
- ¼ cup cornstarch
- 1 teaspoon salt
- 1 teaspoon baking powder
- ½ teaspoon baking soda
- ½ teaspoon ground cinnamon
- ½ teaspoon ground nutmeg
- 1 cup granulated sugar
- 2 eggs
- ¼ cup (½ stick) butter, melted
- ¼ cup applesauce
- 1½ teaspoons vanilla, divided
- ½ cup buttermilk
- Vegetable oil for frying
- ½ cup milk
- 1 cup semisweet or dark chocolate chips
- 1½ to 2 cups powdered sugar, sifted
- Multicolored sprinkles

1. Combine flour, cocoa, cornstarch, salt, baking powder, baking soda, cinnamon and nutmeg in large bowl; mix well.
2. Beat granulated sugar and eggs in large bowl with electric mixer at high speed 3 minutes or until pale and thick. Stir in butter, applesauce and 1 teaspoon vanilla. Add flour mixture alternately with buttermilk, beating at low speed after each addition. Press plastic wrap directly onto surface of dough; refrigerate at least 1 hour.
3. Pour about 2 inches oil into Dutch oven or large heavy saucepan; clip deep-fry or candy thermometer to side of pan. Heat over medium-high heat to 360° to 370°F.
4. Meanwhile, generously flour work surface. Turn out dough onto work surface; dust top with flour. Roll dough to about ¼-inch thickness; cut out doughnuts with floured doughnut cutter. Gather and reroll scraps. Line large wire rack with paper towels.
5. Working in batches, add doughnuts to hot oil (do not crowd pan). Cook 1 minute per side or until golden brown, adjusting heat to maintain temperature during frying. Cool on wire racks.
6. Heat milk in small saucepan until bubbles form around edge of pan. Remove from heat. Add chocolate chips; let stand 1 minute to soften. Add remaining ½ teaspoon vanilla; whisk until smooth. Whisk in enough powdered sugar to form stiff glaze. Dip tops of doughnuts in glaze; top with sprinkles. Let stand until glaze is set.

Peanut Butter Chocolate Chip Bread

MAKES 1 LOAF

- 1½ cups all-purpose flour
- 2 teaspoons baking powder
- ¼ teaspoon salt
- ¼ teaspoon ground cinnamon
- ¼ teaspoon ground nutmeg
- ⅔ cup milk
- 1 teaspoon vanilla
- ¾ cup packed dark brown sugar
- ½ cup vegetable oil
- ½ cup creamy peanut butter
- 2 eggs
- 1 cup finely chopped roasted salted peanuts
- 1 cup mini semisweet chocolate chips

1. Preheat oven to 350°F. Spray 9×5-inch loaf pan with nonstick cooking spray or line with parchment paper.
2. Combine flour, baking powder, salt, cinnamon and nutmeg in medium bowl; mix well. Combine milk and vanilla in small bowl or measuring cup.
3. Beat brown sugar, oil and peanut butter in large bowl until well blended. Add eggs, one at a time; beat until blended. Alternately add flour mixture and milk mixture in two additions, stirring just until blended. Stir in peanuts and chocolate chips. Spread batter in prepared pan.
4. Bake about 1 hour or until toothpick inserted into center comes out clean. Cool in pan 15 minutes; remove to wire rack to cool completely.

Mini Pain au Chocolate

MAKES 16 ROLLS

- ½ cup sugar, divided
- 1 package (14 ounces) refrigerated pie crusts (2 crusts)
- 1 cup semisweet chocolate chips

1. Preheat oven to 400°F. Line baking sheet with with parchment paper or spray with nonstick cooking spray.
2. Sprinkle 2 tablespoons sugar on cutting board or work surface. Unroll one pie crust over sugar; sprinkle with 2 tablespoons sugar. Using pizza wheel or sharp knife, trim away 1 inch dough from four sides to form square. (Save dough trimmings for another use or discard.)
3. Cut square in half; cut each half crosswise into four pieces to create eight small (4×2-inch) rectangles. Place heaping teaspoon chocolate chips at one short end of each rectangle; roll up. Place rolls, seam side down, on prepared baking sheet. Repeat with remaining sugar, pie crust and chocolate chips.
4. Bake 12 to 14 minutes or until lightly browned. Cool on wire rack 10 minutes. Serve warm or cool completely.

Chocolate Peanut Oatmeal Muffins

MAKES 12 MUFFINS

- 1 cup buttermilk
- 1 cup quick oats
- ¾ cup all-purpose flour
- ¼ cup Dutch process or regular unsweetened cocoa powder
- 1 teaspoon baking powder
- ¾ teaspoon salt
- ½ teaspoon baking soda
- ⅔ cup packed dark brown sugar
- ⅓ cup vegetable oil
- 1 egg
- 1 teaspoon vanilla
- ¾ cup roasted salted peanuts, chopped

1. Preheat oven to 400°F. Line 12 standard (2½-inch) muffin cups with paper baking cups or spray with nonstick cooking spray.
2. Combine buttermilk and oats in medium bowl; mix well. Let stand 15 minutes.
3. Meanwhile, combine flour, cocoa, baking powder, salt and baking soda in small bowl; mix well. Whisk brown sugar, oil, egg and vanilla in large bowl until well blended. Add oat mixture; mix well. Add flour mixture; stir until blended. Stir in peanuts. Spoon batter evenly into prepared muffin cups, filling almost full.
4. Bake 13 to 15 minutes or until toothpick inserted into centers comes out clean. Cool in pan 5 minutes; remove to wire racks. Serve warm or cool completely.

Chocolate Cranberry Pumpkin Pancakes

MAKES 16 PANCAKES

- 2 cups all-purpose flour
- ⅓ cup packed brown sugar
- 2 teaspoons baking powder
- ½ teaspoon salt
- ½ teaspoon ground cinnamon
- ¼ teaspoon baking soda
- ¼ teaspoon ground ginger
- ¼ teaspoon ground nutmeg
- 1½ cups milk
- 2 eggs
- ½ cup canned pumpkin
- ¼ cup vegetable oil
- ½ cup mini semisweet chocolate chips
- ½ cup dried cranberries
- ⅓ cup cinnamon chips
- 1 to 2 teaspoons butter, plus additional for serving
- Maple syrup

1. Combine flour, brown sugar, baking powder, salt, cinnamon, baking soda, ginger and nutmeg in large bowl; mix well.
2. Whisk milk, eggs, pumpkin and oil in medium bowl until well blended. Add to flour mixture with chocolate chips, cranberries and cinnamon chips; stir just until dry ingredients are moistened.
3. Heat 1 teaspoon butter on griddle over medium heat. Pour batter by ¼ cupfuls onto griddle. Cook about 3 minutes or until bubbles form on top and bottom of pancakes are lightly browned. Turn pancakes; cook 2 minutes or until browned and cooked through. Repeat with remaining batter, adding additional butter to griddle if necessary. Serve pancakes with maple syrup and additional butter, if desired.

Banana Chocolate Chip Muffins

MAKES 15 MUFFINS

- 2 cups all-purpose flour
- ¼ cup granulated sugar
- ¼ cup packed brown sugar
- 1½ teaspoons baking powder
- ½ teaspoon salt
- ¼ teaspoon baking soda
- 1 cup mashed ripe bananas (about 2 large or 3 small)
- ½ cup (1 stick) butter, melted
- 2 eggs
- ⅓ cup buttermilk
- 1 teaspoon vanilla
- 1 package (about 11 ounces) semisweet chocolate chips

1. Preheat oven to 375°F. Spray 15 standard (2½-inch) muffin cups with nonstick cooking spray or line with paper baking cups.
2. Combine flour, granulated sugar, brown sugar, baking powder, salt and baking soda in large bowl; mix well.
3. Whisk bananas, butter, eggs, buttermilk and vanilla in medium bowl until well blended. Add to flour mixture; stir just until dry ingredients are moistened. Stir in chocolate chips. Spoon batter evenly into prepared muffin cups, filling almost full. Smooth tops.
4. Bake about 18 minutes or until toothpick inserted into centers comes out clean. Cool in pans 5 minutes; remove to wire racks. Serve warm or cool completely.

Note

If you prefer to use only one 12-cup muffin pan, you can divide the batter evenly among 12 standard muffin cups instead of 15 and fill the cups completely.

Cookie Dough Monkey Bread

MAKES ABOUT 16 SERVINGS

- 1 package (about 16 ounces) break-apart refrigerated chocolate chip cookie dough (24 cookies)
- 2 packages (7½ ounces each) refrigerated buttermilk biscuits (10 biscuits per package)
- 1 cup semisweet chocolate chips, divided
- ¼ cup whipping cream

1. Preheat oven to 350°F. Generously spray 12-cup (10-inch) bundt pan with nonstick cooking spray.
2. Break cookie dough into 24 pieces; split each piece in half to create total of 48 pieces. Separate biscuits; cut each biscuit into four pieces with scissors.
3. Layer half of cookie dough and half of biscuit pieces in prepared pan, alternating doughs. Sprinkle with ¼ cup chocolate chips. Repeat layers with remaining cookie dough and biscuit pieces; sprinkle with ¼ cup chocolate chips.
4. Bake 27 to 30 minutes or until biscuits are golden brown, covering pan loosely with foil during last 10 minutes of baking. Remove pan to wire rack; let stand, covered, 5 minutes. Loosen edges of bread with knife; invert onto serving plate.
5. Pour cream into medium microwavable bowl; microwave on HIGH 1 minute or until simmering. Add remaining ½ cup chocolate chips; stir until chocolate is melted. Let stand 5 minutes to thicken slightly. Drizzle glaze over bread.

Peanut Butter and Chocolate Swirls

MAKES 12 SERVINGS

- 1 container (8 ounces) crescent roll dough sheet
- ⅔ cup semisweet chocolate chips
- 3½ tablespoons whipping cream, divided
- ⅓ cup plus 2 tablespoons peanut butter, divided
- ¼ cup packed brown sugar
- ¼ cup finely chopped roasted peanuts

1. Preheat oven to 350°F. Spray 12 standard (2½-inch) muffin cups with nonstick cooking spray.
2. Unroll crescent roll dough on work surface. Combine chocolate chips and 2 tablespoons cream in medium microwavable bowl; microwave on HIGH 30 seconds. Stir until chocolate is melted and mixture is smooth. Place ⅓ cup peanut butter in small microwavable bowl; microwave on HIGH 20 seconds or just until softened.
3. Spread softened peanut butter over dough to within ½ inch of edges; sprinkle with brown sugar, pressing lightly into peanut butter. Spread two thirds of chocolate mixture over brown sugar; sprinkle with peanuts. Roll up tightly jelly-roll style; pinch seam to seal. Make sure roll is 12 inches long before cutting crosswise into 1-inch slices. Place slices cut sides up in prepared muffin cups.
4. Bake 12 minutes or until golden brown. Cool in pan 2 minutes; use small spatula or knife to loosen edges. Remove to wire rack set over sheet of waxed paper.
5. Add remaining 1½ tablespoons cream to remaining chocolate mixture; microwave on HIGH 10 to 20 seconds or until mixture is smooth and thinned to glaze consistency. Place remaining 2 tablespoons peanut butter in small microwavable bowl; microwave on HIGH 30 seconds or until melted. Drizzle chocolate glaze and peanut butter over rolls. Serve warm or at room temperature.

Triple Chocolate Sticky Buns

MAKES 12 BUNS

Dough

- 2⅔ cups bread flour
- ⅓ cup unsweetened cocoa powder
- ¼ cup granulated sugar
- 1 package (¼ ounce) instant yeast
- 1 teaspoon salt
- ½ cup sour cream
- 1 egg
- ¼ cup warm water (130°F)
- 3 tablespoons butter, softened

Topping

- ⅓ cup packed brown sugar
- ¼ cup (½ stick) butter
- 2 tablespoons light corn syrup
- 1 tablespoon unsweetened cocoa powder

Filling

- ⅓ cup packed brown sugar
- ½ teaspoon ground cinnamon
- 3 tablespoons butter, melted
- ⅔ cup chopped walnuts, toasted*
- ½ cup semisweet chocolate chips

**To toast walnuts, spread on baking sheet. Bake in preheated 350°F oven 6 to 8 minutes or until lightly browned and fragrant, stirring frequently.*

1. Combine flour, cocoa, ¼ cup granulated sugar, yeast and salt in large bowl of stand mixer. Whisk sour cream and egg in small bowl until well blended. Add water, softened butter and sour cream mixture to flour mixture; beat with paddle attachment at medium speed 3 minutes.
2. Replace paddle attachment with dough hook; mix at medium-low speed about 6 minutes. Place dough in greased bowl; turn to grease top. Cover and let rise in warm place about 40 minutes. (Dough will not double in size.)
3. Meanwhile, prepare topping and filling. Spray 9-inch round cake pan with nonstick cooking spray. Combine ⅓ cup brown sugar, ¼ cup butter, corn syrup and 1 tablespoon cocoa in small saucepan; heat over medium heat until brown sugar dissolves and mixture bubbles around edge, stirring frequently. Pour into prepared pan. Combine ⅓ cup brown sugar and cinnamon in small bowl; mix well.
4. Roll out dough into 12×8-inch rectangle on lightly floured surface. Brush with melted butter and sprinkle with brown sugar mixture. Sprinkle with walnuts and chocolate chips; gently press filling into dough. Starting with long side, roll up tightly jelly-roll style; pinch seam to seal. Cut crosswise into 12 slices; arrange slices cut sides up over topping in pan. Cover and let rise in warm place about 35 minutes or until doubled in size. Preheat oven to 375°F.
5. Bake about 25 minutes or just until buns in center of pan are firm to the touch. Immediately invert onto serving plate. Serve warm or at room temperature.

Chocolate Chip Elvis Bread

MAKES 4 MINI LOAVES

- 2½ cups all-purpose flour
- ½ cup granulated sugar
- ½ cup packed brown sugar
- 1 tablespoon baking powder
- ¾ teaspoon salt
- 1 cup mashed ripe bananas (about 2 large)
- 1 cup milk
- ¾ cup peanut butter
- ¼ cup vegetable oil
- 1 egg, lightly beaten
- 1 teaspoon vanilla
- 1¼ cups semisweet chocolate chips

1. Preheat oven to 350°F. Spray four mini (5½×3-inch) or one 9×5-inch loaf pan with nonstick cooking spray.
2. Combine flour, granulated sugar, brown sugar, baking powder and salt in large bowl; mix well. Whisk bananas, milk, peanut butter, oil, egg and vanilla in medium bowl until well blended. Add to flour mixture with chocolate chips; stir just until dry ingredients are moistened. Pour batter into prepared pans.
3. Bake about 40 minutes or until toothpick inserted into centers comes out clean (65 to 75 minutes for 9×5-inch pan). Cool in pans 10 minutes; remove to wire racks to cool completely.

White Chocolate Chunk Muffins

MAKES 12 JUMBO MUFFINS

- 2½ cups all-purpose flour
- 1 cup packed brown sugar
- ⅓ cup unsweetened cocoa powder
- 2 teaspoons baking soda
- ½ teaspoon salt
- 1⅓ cups buttermilk
- 6 tablespoons (¾ stick) butter, melted
- 2 eggs, beaten
- 1½ teaspoons vanilla
- 1½ cups chopped white chocolate

1. Preheat oven to 400°F. Spray 12 jumbo (3½-inch) muffin cups with nonstick cooking spray.
2. Combine flour, brown sugar, cocoa, baking soda and salt in large bowl; mix well. Whisk buttermilk, butter, eggs and vanilla in small bowl until blended. Add to flour mixture; stir just until dry ingredients are moistened. Fold in white chocolate. Spoon batter into prepared muffin cups, filling about half full.
3. Bake 25 to 30 minutes or until toothpick inserted into centers comes out clean. Cool in pans 5 minutes; remove to wire racks to cool 10 minutes. Serve warm or cool completely.

Chocolate Chip Scones

MAKES 24 SCONES

- **2 cups all-purpose flour**
- **1 cup mini semisweet chocolate chips**
- **¾ cup golden raisins**
- **½ cup sugar**
- **2 teaspoons baking powder**
- **¼ teaspoon baking soda**
- **¼ teaspoon salt**
- **¼ teaspoon ground cinnamon**
- **½ cup (1 stick) butter, cut into small pieces**
- **½ cup buttermilk**
- **2 eggs, divided**
- **½ teaspoon vanilla**
- **1 tablespoon milk**

1. Preheat oven to 350°F. Line two baking sheets with parchment paper or spray with nonstick cooking spray.
2. Combine flour, chocolate chips, raisins, sugar, baking powder, baking soda, salt and cinnamon in large bowl; mix well.
3. Cut in butter with pastry blender or two knives until mixture resembles coarse crumbs. Whisk buttermilk, 1 egg and vanilla in small bowl until blended. Add to flour mixture; stir just until sticky dough forms.
4. Using 2 tablespoons dough for each scone, drop dough onto prepared baking sheets. Whisk remaining egg and milk in small bowl; brush over tops of scones.
5. Bake 12 to 14 minutes or until toothpick inserted into centers comes out clean. Cool on wire rack 5 minutes. Serve warm.

Little Chocolate Chip Coffeecakes

MAKES 18 COFFEECAKES

- 1⅓ cups all-purpose flour
- ¾ teaspoon baking powder
- ½ teaspoon salt
- ¼ teaspoon baking soda
- ¾ cup packed brown sugar
- ½ cup (1 stick) butter, softened
- ¼ cup granulated sugar
- 1 teaspoon vanilla
- 2 eggs
- ½ cup plus 3 tablespoons milk, divided
- 1½ cups semisweet chocolate chips, divided

1. Preheat oven to 350°F. Generously grease and flour 18 mini (¼-cup) bundt cups.
2. Combine flour, baking powder, salt and baking soda in small bowl; mix well.
3. Beat brown sugar, butter, granulated sugar and vanilla in large bowl with electric mixer at medium speed about 3 minutes or until light and fluffy. Beat in eggs, one at a time, until well blended. Alternately add flour mixture and ½ cup milk, beginning and ending with flour mixture; beat at low speed until blended. Stir in 1 cup chocolate chips.
4. Spoon batter into prepared bundt cups, filling three-fourths full (about 3 tablespoons batter per cup).
5. Bake about 16 minutes or until toothpick inserted into centers comes out clean. Cool in pans 5 minutes; invert onto wire racks to cool completely.
6. Combine remaining ½ cup chocolate chips and 3 tablespoons milk in small microwavable bowl; microwave on HIGH 30 seconds. Stir; microwave at 15-second intervals until chocolate is melted and mixture is smooth. Drizzle glaze over cakes.

Pumpkin Chocolate Chip Muffins

MAKES 18 MUFFINS

- 2½ cups all-purpose flour
- 1 tablespoon baking powder
- 1½ teaspoons pumpkin pie spice*
- ½ teaspoon salt
- 1 cup canned pumpkin
- 1 cup packed brown sugar
- ¾ cup milk
- 6 tablespoons (¾ stick) butter, melted
- 2 eggs
- 1 cup semisweet chocolate chips
- ½ cup chopped walnuts

**Or substitute ¾ teaspoon ground cinnamon, ½ teaspoon ground ginger and ¼ teaspoon each ground allspice and ground nutmeg.*

1. Preheat oven to 400°F. Line 18 standard (2½-inch) muffin cups with paper baking cups or spray with nonstick cooking spray.
2. Combine flour, baking powder, pumpkin pie spice and salt in large bowl; mix well.
3. Whisk pumpkin, brown sugar, milk, butter and eggs in medium bowl until well blended. Add pumpkin mixture, chocolate chips and walnuts to flour mixture; stir just until dry ingredients are moistened. Spoon batter evenly into prepared muffin cups, filling two-thirds full.
4. Bake 15 minutes or until toothpick inserted into centers comes out clean. Cool in pans 10 minutes; remove to wire racks to cool completely.

Exceptional Cookies

Perfect Chocolate Chip Cookies

MAKES ABOUT 16 COOKIES

- **2 cups all-purpose flour**
- **1 teaspoon baking soda**
- **½ teaspoon salt**
- **¾ cup (1½ sticks) butter, softened**
- **¾ cup packed brown sugar**
- **½ cup granulated sugar**
- **1 egg**
- **1¼ teaspoons vanilla**
- **8 ounces chocolate chips or bittersweet chocolate, chopped**
- **Flaky sea salt (optional)**

1. Combine flour, baking soda and ½ teaspoon salt in medium bowl; mix well.
2. Beat butter, brown sugar and granulated sugar in large bowl with electric mixer at medium-high speed about 3 minutes or until light and fluffy. Add egg and vanilla; beat until blended. Add flour mixture; beat at low speed until blended. Stir in chocolate chips. If desired, cover dough and refrigerate up to 2 days.
3. Preheat oven to 350°F. Line cookie sheets with parchment paper. For each cookie, shape about 2 tablespoons of dough into a ball; place on prepared cookie sheets. Sprinkle with sea salt, if desired.
4. Bake 12 minutes or until edges are lightly browned. Cool on cookie sheets 5 minutes; remove to wire racks to cool completely.

Chocolate Coconut Toffee Delights

MAKES 1 DOZEN LARGE COOKIES

- ½ cup all-purpose flour
- ¼ teaspoon baking powder
- ¼ teaspoon salt
- 1 package (12 ounces) semisweet chocolate chips, divided
- ¼ cup (½ stick) butter, cut into small pieces
- ¾ cup packed brown sugar
- 2 eggs
- 1 teaspoon vanilla
- 1½ cups flaked coconut
- 1 cup toffee baking bits
- ½ cup bittersweet chocolate chips

1. Preheat oven to 350°F. Line cookie sheets with parchment paper. Combine flour, baking powder and salt in small bowl; mix well.
2. Combine 1 cup semisweet chocolate chips and butter in medium microwavable bowl; microwave on HIGH 1 minute. Stir; microwave at additional 20-second intervals until mixture is melted and smooth, stirring after each interval.
3. Beat brown sugar, eggs and vanilla in large bowl with electric mixer at medium speed 2 to 3 minutes or until creamy. Beat in chocolate mixture until well blended. Add flour mixture; beat at low speed until blended. Stir in coconut, toffee bits and remaining 1 cup semisweet chocolate chips. Drop dough by heaping ⅓ cupfuls 3 inches apart onto prepared cookie sheets. Flatten into 3½-inch circles with spatula.
4. Bake 15 to 17 minutes or until edges are firm to the touch. Cool on cookie sheets 2 minutes; slide parchment paper and cookies onto wire racks to cool completely.
5. Place bittersweet chocolate chips in small microwavable bowl; mcrowave on HIGH 30 seconds. Stir; microwave at additional 20-second intervals until chocolate is melted, stirring after each interval. Drizzle chocolate over cookies; let stand until set.

Chocolate Hazelnut Sandwich Cookies

MAKES 2½ DOZEN SANDWICH COOKIES

- **¾ cup (1½ sticks) butter, softened**
- **¾ cup sugar**
- **3 egg yolks**
- **1 teaspoon vanilla**
- **2 cups all-purpose flour**
- **¼ teaspoon salt**
- **⅔ cup chocolate hazelnut spread**

1. Beat butter and sugar in large bowl with electric mixer at medium speed 1 minute. Beat in egg yolks and vanilla until well blended. Add flour and salt; beat at low speed just until combined.
2. Divide dough in half. Shape each piece into 6×1½-inch log. Wrap in plastic wrap; refrigerate at least 2 hours or until firm.
3. Preheat oven to 350°F. Line cookie sheets with parchment paper. Cut dough into ⅛-inch-thick slices; place 1 inch apart on prepared cookie sheets.
4. Bake 10 to 12 minutes or until edges are lightly browned. Cool on cookie sheets 5 minutes; remove to wire racks to cool completely.
5. Spread 1 teaspoon chocolate hazelnut spread on flat side of half of cookies; top with remaining cookies.

Note

The dough can be refrigerated up to 3 days or frozen for up to 1 month.

Dark Chocolate Dreams

MAKES 14 LARGE COOKIES

- ½ cup all-purpose flour
- ¾ teaspoon espresso powder *or* ¼ teaspoon ground cinnamon
- ½ teaspoon baking powder
- ¼ teaspoon salt
- 16 ounces bittersweet chocolate, coarsely chopped
- ¼ cup (½ stick) butter, softened
- 1½ cups sugar
- 3 eggs
- 1 teaspoon vanilla
- 1 package (12 ounces) white chocolate chips
- 1 cup dark chocolate chips

1. Preheat oven to 350°F. Spray cookie sheets with nonstick cooking spray or line with parchment paper.
2. Combine flour, espresso powder, baking powder and salt in small bowl; mix well.
3. Combine chocolate and butter in large microwavable bowl; microwave on HIGH 2 minutes. Stir; microwave 1 to 2 minutes or until chocolate is melted, stirring after 1 minute. Cool slightly.
4. Beat sugar, eggs and vanilla in large bowl with electric mixer at medium-high speed about 6 minutes or until very thick and light in color. Reduce speed to low; slowly beat in chocolate mixture until well blended. Gradually beat in flour mixture just until blended. Stir in white and dark chocolate chips.
5. Drop dough by level ⅓ cupfuls 3 inches apart onto prepared cookie sheets. Flatten into 4-inch circles with moistened fingers.
6. Bake 12 minutes or just until firm and surface begins to crack. *Do not overbake.* Cool on cookie sheets 5 minutes; remove to wire racks to cool completely.

Cocoa Spice Cookies

MAKES ABOUT 5 DOZEN COOKIES

- 2½ cups all-purpose flour
- ½ cup unsweetened Dutch process cocoa powder
- 1 teaspoon ground cinnamon
- 1 teaspoon ground cardamom
- ½ teaspoon baking soda
- ½ teaspoon salt
- 1½ cups packed dark brown sugar
- 1 cup (2 sticks) butter, softened
- 2 egg yolks
- 1 teaspoon coconut extract
- Demerara sugar or coarse decorating sugar

1. Combine flour, cocoa, cinnamon, cardamom, baking soda and salt in medium bowl; mix well.
2. Beat brown sugar and butter in large bowl with electric mixer at medium speed about 3 minutes or until light and fluffy. Beat in egg yolks and coconut extract. Gradually add flour mixture at low speed, beating just until blended.
3. Spread demerara sugar evenly on waxed paper. Divide dough into four pieces; shape each piece into 6-inch log. Roll logs in sugar, coating evenly. Wrap logs in plastic wrap; refrigerate 3 to 4 hours or until firm.
4. Preheat oven to 325°F. Line cookie sheets with parchment paper. Cut each log into 16 slices; place 1 inch apart on prepared cookie sheets.
5. Bake 12 minutes. Cool on cookie sheets 5 minutes; remove to wire racks to cool completely.

Mexican Chocolate Macaroons

MAKES ABOUT 2 DOZEN COOKIES

- **8 ounces semisweet chocolate, divided**
- **1¾ cups plus ⅓ cup whole almonds, divided**
- **¾ cup sugar**
- **½ teaspoon salt**
- **2 egg whites**
- **1 teaspoon ground cinnamon**
- **1 teaspoon vanilla**

1. Preheat oven to 400°F. Line cookie sheets with parchment paper or spray with nonstick cooking spray.
2. Place 5 ounces chocolate in food processor; process until coarsely chopped. Add 1¾ cups almonds, sugar and salt; pulse until finely ground. Add egg whites, cinnamon and vanilla; process just until mixture forms moist dough.
3. Shape dough into 1-inch balls. (Dough will be sticky.) Place 2 inches apart on prepared cookie sheets. Press 1 whole almond into center of each dough ball.
4. Bake 8 to 10 minutes or just until set. Cool on cookie sheets 2 minutes; remove to wire racks to cool completely.
5. Chop remaining 3 ounces chocolate; melt in microwave or on stovetop. Place in small resealable food storage bag. Cut off small corner of bag; drizzle chocolate over cookies. Let stand until set.

Cocoa Crinkle Sandwiches

MAKES ABOUT 20 SANDWICH COOKIES

Cookies

- **1¾ cups all-purpose flour**
- **½ cup unsweetened cocoa powder**
- **1 teaspoon baking soda**
- **½ teaspoon salt**
- **½ cup (1 stick) butter**
- **1½ cups granulated sugar, divided**
- **2 eggs**
- **2 teaspoons vanilla**

Frosting

- **2½ cups powdered sugar**
- **1 cup (2 sticks) butter, softened**
- **2 tablespoons unsweetened cocoa powder**
- **½ cup dark chocolate chips, melted and cooled**
- **3 tablespoons whipping cream**
- **1 teaspoon vanilla**
- **⅛ teaspoon salt**

1. For cookies, combine flour, ½ cup cocoa, baking soda and ½ teaspoon salt in medium bowl; mix well.
2. Melt ½ cup butter in large saucepan over medium heat; cool slightly. Add 1¼ cups granulated sugar; whisk until smooth. Whisk in eggs, one at a time, until blended. Whisk in 2 teaspoons vanilla until smooth. Add flour mixture; stir just until blended. Cover with plastic wrap; refrigerate 2 hours.
3. Preheat oven to 350°F. Line cookie sheets with parchment paper. Shape dough into 1-inch balls. Place remaining ¼ cup granulated sugar in shallow bowl; roll balls in sugar to coat. Place 1½ inches apart on prepared cookie sheets.
4. Bake 12 minutes or until set. Cool on cookie sheets 5 minutes; remove to wire racks to cool completely.
5. For frosting, beat powdered sugar, 1 cup butter and 2 tablespoons cocoa in large bowl with electric mixer at medium-low speed until blended. Add melted chocolate, cream, 1 teaspoon vanilla and ⅛ teaspoon salt; beat until blended. Increase speed to medium-high; beat about 5 minutes or until frosting is very fluffy.
6. Pipe or spread about 2 tablespoons frosting on flat sides of half of cookies; top with remaining cookies. Store leftovers in refrigerator.

Chocolate Chunk Pizza Cookie

MAKES 3 PIZZA COOKIES (2 TO 3 SERVINGS EACH)

- 2 cups all-purpose flour
- 1 teaspoon baking soda
- 1 teaspoon salt
- ¾ cup (1½ sticks) butter, softened
- 1 cup packed brown sugar
- ¼ cup granulated sugar
- 2 eggs
- 1 teaspoon vanilla
- 1 package (12 ounces) semisweet chocolate chunks or chips
- Vanilla ice cream

1. Preheat oven to 400°F. Spray three 6-inch cast iron skillets, cake pans or deep-dish pizza pans with nonstick cooking spray.*

2. Combine flour, baking soda and salt in medium bowl; mix well. Beat butter, brown sugar and granulated sugar in large bowl with electric mixer at medium speed about 3 minutes or until creamy. Beat in eggs and vanilla until well blended. Gradually beat in flour mixture at low speed just until blended. Stir in chocolate chunks. Spread dough evenly in prepared skillets.

3. Bake about 15 minutes or until top and edges are deep golden brown but center is still slightly soft. Top with ice cream. Serve warm.

**If you don't have three small skillets or pans, you can bake one cookie at a time. Refrigerate dough between batches and make sure skillet is completely cool before adding more dough. (Clean and spray skillet again before adding each new batch.)*

Double Chocolate Brownie Cookies

MAKES 3 DOZEN COOKIES

- **1 package (12 ounces) semisweet or dark chocolate chips, divided**
- **1⅔ cups all-purpose flour**
- **½ teaspoon baking soda**
- **½ teaspoon salt**
- **½ cup (1 stick) butter, softened**
- **½ cup packed brown sugar**
- **¼ cup granulated sugar**
- **2 eggs**
- **¾ teaspoon vanilla**
- **¾ cup chopped walnuts (optional)**

1. Preheat oven to 350°F. Line cookie sheets with parchment paper.
2. Place ¾ cup chocolate chips in small microwavable bowl; microwave on LOW (30% power) 2 minutes. Stir; microwave 1 minute or until chocolate is melted. Set aside to cool slightly.
3. Combine flour, baking soda and salt in medium bowl; mix well.
4. Beat butter, brown sugar and granulated sugar in large bowl with electric mixer at medium speed about 3 minutes or until light and creamy. Add eggs, one at a time, beating well and scraping down side of bowl after each addition. Beat in vanilla. Add melted chocolate; beat until well blended. Gradually add flour mixture at low speed, beating just until blended. Stir in remaining chocolate chips and walnuts, if desired. Drop dough by tablespoonfuls onto prepared cookie sheets.
5. Bake 8 minutes or just until edges of cookies are set but centers are still soft. Cool on cookie sheets 2 minutes; remove to wire racks to cool completely.

Chocolate Peanut Butter Drops

MAKES ABOUT 4 DOZEN COOKIES

- 1⅓ cups all-purpose flour
- ½ cup unsweetened cocoa powder
- ¾ teaspoon baking soda
- ¼ teaspoon salt
- ¾ cup (1½ sticks) butter, softened
- ½ cup granulated sugar
- ½ cup packed brown sugar
- 1 egg
- 2 tablespoons water
- ½ teaspoon vanilla
- 1 package (12 ounces) peanut butter chips

1. Preheat oven to 375°F. Combine flour, cocoa, baking soda and salt in medium bowl; mix well.
2. Beat butter, granulated sugar and brown sugar in large bowl with electric mixer at medium speed 2 to 3 minutes or until creamy. Add egg, water and vanilla; beat 2 minutes. Add flour mixture; beat at low speed until well blended. Stir in peanut butter chips. Drop dough by rounded tablespoonfuls 3 inches apart onto ungreased cookie sheets.
3. Bake 8 to 10 minutes or until set. Remove to wire racks to cool completely.

No-Bake Cocoa Oatmeal Cookies

MAKES 2 DOZEN COOKIES

- 1 cup sugar
- 1 cup flaked coconut
- ½ cup unsweetened cocoa powder
- ½ cup creamy peanut butter
- ½ cup milk
- ½ teaspoon vanilla
- 2 cups old-fashioned oats

1. Line cookie sheet with parchment paper.
2. Combine sugar, coconut, cocoa, peanut butter, milk and vanilla in medium saucepan; bring to a boil over medium-high heat. Reduce heat to low; stir in oats until well blended.
3. Drop dough by tablespoonfuls onto prepared cookie sheet. Freeze 1 to 2 hours. Store in refrigerator.

Chocolate Caramel Thumbprints

MAKES 2½ DOZEN COOKIES

Cookies

- 1½ cups all-purpose flour
- ¾ cup unsweetened cocoa powder
- ½ teaspoon salt
- 1 cup (2 sticks) butter, softened
- ⅔ cup packed brown sugar
- 2 eggs, separated
- 1 teaspoon vanilla
- 2 cups finely chopped pecans

Caramel Filling

- ½ cup packed brown sugar
- ¼ cup (½ stick) butter
- 2 tablespoons whipping cream
- Pinch of salt
- 2 tablespoons powdered sugar

1. For cookies, preheat oven to 375°F. Line cookie sheets with parchment paper or leave ungreased.
2. Combine flour, cocoa and ½ teaspoon salt in small bowl; mix well.
3. Beat butter and ⅔ cup brown sugar in large bowl with electric mixer at medium speed about 3 minutes or until light and fluffy. Beat in egg yolks and vanilla until well blended. Gradually beat in flour mixture at low speed just until blended. Shape level tablespoonfuls of dough into balls.
4. Whisk egg whites in small bowl. Place pecans in medium bowl. Dip balls one at a time into egg whites, turning to coat completely and letting excess drip back into bowl. Roll in pecans to coat. Place on prepared cookie sheets. Press thumb firmly into center of each cookie.
5. Bake about 10 minutes until cookies are set. Quickly repress thumbprints with end of wooden spoon. Cool on cookie sheets 5 minutes; remove to wire racks to cool completely.
6. For filling, combine ½ cup brown sugar and ¼ cup butter in small saucepan; cook over medium heat until mixture begins to boil, stirring constantly. Boil 1 minute, stirring constantly. Remove from heat; stir in cream and pinch of salt. Cool 15 minutes; whisk in powdered sugar until smooth. Fill each cookie with about ½ teaspoon filling; let stand until firm.

Ultimate White and Dark Chocolate Chippers

MAKES ABOUT 5 DOZEN COOKIES

- 1 cup (2 sticks) butter, softened
- ¾ cup granulated sugar
- ¾ cup packed brown sugar
- 2 eggs
- 2 tablespoons almond-flavored liqueur or water
- 1 teaspoon baking soda
- 1 teaspoon vanilla
- ¼ teaspoon salt
- 2⅓ cups all-purpose flour
- 1 cup semisweet chocolate chips
- 1 cup white chocolate chips
- 1 cup coarsely chopped pecans

1. Preheat oven to 375°F. Line cookie sheets with parchment paper or leave ungreased.
2. Beat butter, granulated sugar, brown sugar, eggs, liqueur, baking soda, vanilla and salt in large bowl with electric mixer about 3 minutes or until light and fluffy. Add flour; stir until dough is smooth and stiff. Stir in semisweet chips, white chocolate chips and pecans. Drop dough by teaspoonfuls 2 inches apart onto prepared cookie sheets.
3. Bake 8 to 10 minutes or until cookies are just set in center and edges are lightly browned. Remove to wire racks to cool completely.

Super Chocolate Cookies

MAKES ABOUT 20 LARGE COOKIES

- 2 cups all-purpose flour
- ⅓ cup unsweetened cocoa powder
- 1 teaspoon baking soda
- ½ teaspoon salt
- 1⅓ cups packed brown sugar
- 1 cup (2 sticks) butter, softened
- 2 eggs
- 2 teaspoons vanilla
- 1 cup candy-coated chocolate pieces
- 1 cup dried cranberries, dried cherries and/or raisins
- ¾ cup salted peanuts, chopped

1. Preheat oven to 350°F. Combine flour, cocoa, baking soda and salt in medium bowl; mix well.
2. Beat brown sugar and butter in large bowl with electric mixer at medium speed about 4 minutes or until light and fluffy. Add eggs and vanilla; beat until well blended. Gradually add flour mixture; beat at low speed until blended. Stir in chocolate pieces, cranberries and peanuts.
3. Drop dough by ¼ cupfuls 3 inches apart onto ungreased cookie sheets. Flatten slightly with fingertips.
4. Bake 13 to 15 minutes or until almost set. Cool on cookie sheets 2 minutes; remove to wire racks to cool completely.

Chocolate Chip Sandwich Cookies

MAKES 16 SANDWICH COOKIES

- ¾ cup plus ⅓ cup packed brown sugar
- ½ cup (1 stick) butter, softened
- 1 egg
- 1 teaspoon vanilla
- ¾ teaspoon baking soda
- ½ teaspoon salt
- 1¾ cups all-purpose flour
- 3 cups semisweet chocolate chips, divided
- 6 tablespoons whipping cream

1. Preheat oven to 350°F. Line cookie sheets with parchment paper.
2. Beat brown sugar and butter in large bowl with electric mixer at medium speed 5 minutes or until light and fluffy. Add egg and vanilla; beat until well blended. Beat in baking soda and salt. Slowly add flour, beating at low speed until blended. Stir in 1½ cups chocolate chips. Drop dough by heaping tablespoonfuls 2 inches apart onto prepared cookie sheets.
3. Bake about 10 minutes or until cookies are just beginning to brown around edges but are still very soft in center. (Cookies will look underbaked.) Cool on cookie sheets 5 minutes; remove to wire racks to cool completely.
4. While cookies are baking, prepare chocolate filling. Heat cream to a simmer in microwave or on stovetop. Add remaining 1½ cups chocolate chips to cream; let stand 1 minute. Stir until smooth. Refrigerate 1 hour, stirring occasionally. (Filling should be thick enough to spread and still be shiny when stirred.)
5. Spread heaping tablespoonful of filling onto bottoms of half of cookies; top with remaining cookies.

Cocoa Hazelnut Macaroons

MAKES 3 DOZEN COOKIES

- ⅓ cup hazelnuts
- ¾ cup quick oats
- 6 tablespoons unsweetened cocoa powder
- ⅓ cup packed brown sugar
- 2 tablespoons all-purpose flour
- 4 egg whites
- 1 teaspoon vanilla
- ½ teaspoon salt
- ⅓ cup plus 1 tablespoon granulated sugar

1. Preheat oven to 375°F. Spread hazelnuts in even layer on cookie sheet. Bake 8 minutes or until lightly browned. *Reduce oven temperature to 325°F.*
2. Quickly transfer nuts to clean dry dish towel. Fold towel; rub vigorously to remove as much of the skins as possible.
3. Finely chop nuts using chef's knife or food processor. Combine chopped nuts, oats, cocoa, brown sugar and flour in medium bowl; mix well.
4. Beat egg whites, vanilla and salt in medium bowl with electric mixer at high speed until soft peaks form. Gradually add granulated sugar; beat at high speed until stiff peaks form. Gently fold in nut mixture with rubber spatula. Drop dough by level tablespoonfuls onto ungreased cookie sheets.
5. Bake 15 to 17 minutes or until tops of cookies no longer appear wet. Remove to wire racks to cool completely. Store in loosely covered container.

Deep Dark Chocolate Drops

MAKES ABOUT 3 DOZEN COOKIES

- **1¼ cups all-purpose flour**
- **¼ cup unsweetened cocoa powder**
- **½ teaspoon baking soda**
- **½ teaspoon salt**
- **1½ cups semisweet chocolate chips, divided**
- **½ cup (1 stick) butter, softened**
- **½ cup granulated sugar**
- **¼ cup packed brown sugar**
- **1 egg**
- **2 tablespoons milk**
- **1 teaspoon vanilla**

1. Preheat oven to 350°F. Line cookie sheets with parchment paper or spray with nonstick cooking spray.
2. Combine flour, cocoa, baking soda and salt in medium bowl; mix well.
3. Place ½ cup chocolate chips in small microwavable bowl; microwave on HIGH 1 minute. Stir; microwave at additional 30-second intervals until chocolate is melted, stirring after each interval. Set aside to cool slightly.
4. Beat butter, granulated sugar and brown sugar in large bowl with electric mixer at medium speed about 3 minutes or until light and fluffy. Add egg, milk, vanilla and melted chocolate; beat until well blended. Gradually add flour mixture at low speed, beating just until blended. Stir in remaining 1 cup chocolate chips. Drop dough by rounded tablespoonfuls 2 inches apart onto prepared cookie sheets.
5. Bake 10 minutes or until cookies are set. Cool on cookie sheets 2 minutes; remove to wire racks to cool completely.

Brownies and Bars

Chocolate Chip Brownie

MAKES 8 TO 10 SERVINGS

- ¾ cup all-purpose flour
- ½ cup unsweetened Dutch process cocoa powder
- ½ teaspoon salt
- ½ teaspoon baking powder
- ¾ cup granulated sugar
- ½ cup packed brown sugar
- ½ cup (1 stick) butter, melted
- 2 eggs
- ½ teaspoon vanilla
- 1 cup dark chocolate chips

1. Preheat oven to 350°F. Spray 9-inch round cake pan with nonstick cooking spray. Line bottom with parchment paper; spray paper with cooking spray.
2. Combine flour, cocoa, salt and baking powder in medium bowl; mix well. Whisk granulated sugar, brown sugar and butter in large bowl until well blended. Add eggs, one at a time, whisking until well blended after each addition. Whisk in vanilla until blended. Add flour mixture; stir just until blended. Stir in chocolate chips. Spread batter in prepared pan.
3. Bake 22 to 27 minutes or until brownie is just set to the touch and toothpick inserted into center comes out with fudgy crumbs. Cool in pan on wire rack.
4. To remove from pan, loosen edge with small knife; invert onto wire rack and invert again onto serving plate. Cut into wedges.

Chocolate Pecan Bars

MAKES 2 TO 3 DOZEN BARS

Crust

- 1⅓ cups all-purpose flour
- ½ cup (1 stick) butter, softened
- ¼ cup packed brown sugar
- ½ teaspoon salt

Topping

- ¾ cup light corn syrup
- 3 eggs, lightly beaten
- 2 tablespoons butter, melted
- ½ teaspoon vanilla
- ½ teaspoon almond extract
- ¾ cup granulated sugar
- ¾ cup milk chocolate chips
- ¾ cup semisweet chocolate chips
- ¾ cup chopped pecans, toasted*

**To toast pecans, spread on baking sheet. Bake in preheated 350°F oven 5 to 7 minutes or until lightly browned and fragrant, stirring frequently.*

1. Preheat oven to 350°F. Spray 13×9-inch baking pan with nonstick cooking spray.
2. For crust, combine flour, ½ cup softened butter, brown sugar and salt in medium bowl; mix with fork until crumbly. Press into bottom of prepared pan.
3. Bake crust 12 to 15 minutes or until lightly browned. Cool on wire rack 10 minutes.
4. Meanwhile, for topping, combine corn syrup, eggs, 2 tablespoons melted butter, vanilla and almond extract in large bowl; stir with fork until well blended (do not beat). Stir in granulated sugar, chocolate chips and pecans until blended. Pour over baked crust.
5. Bake 25 to 30 minutes or until toothpick inserted into center comes out clean. Cool completely in pan on wire rack.

Tip

For easy removal of corn syrup, spray the inside of the measuring cup with nonstick cooking spray before measuring.

Super Fudgy Brownies

MAKES 12 TO 16 BROWNIES

- ½ cup all-purpose flour
- ½ cup unsweetened cocoa powder
- ½ teaspoon salt
- ½ cup (1 stick) butter
- 1 cup sugar
- 2 eggs
- 1 teaspoon vanilla
- ¾ cup semisweet or bittersweet chocolate chips

1. Preheat oven to 350°F. Spray 8-inch square baking pan with nonstick cooking spray. Line with parchment paper, leaving overhang on two sides of pan, and spray again.
2. Sift flour, cocoa and salt into small bowl. Melt butter in medium saucepan over medium heat.* Remove from heat; add sugar and whisk 2 minutes. Add eggs and vanilla; whisk 1 minute or until very well blended. Add flour mixture; stir just until blended. Stir in chocolate chips. Spread batter in prepared pan; smooth top.
3. Bake 20 to 22 minutes or until edges are set and toothpick inserted into center comes out with fudgy crumbs. Cool completely in pan on wire rack.

**Or microwave butter in medium bowl until melted; whisk in sugar and proceed with recipe as directed.*

Chocolate Oat Dream Bars

MAKES 12 TO 16 BARS

- **2¼ cups all-purpose flour**
- **1 cup plus 2 tablespoons packed brown sugar**
- **1 cup plus 2 tablespoons old-fashioned oats**
- **¾ teaspoon baking soda**
- **½ teaspoon salt**
- **1 cup plus 2 tablespoons (2¼ sticks) butter, melted**
- **1 teaspoon vanilla**
- **3 tablespoons caramel sauce**
- **¾ cup semisweet chocolate chips**

1. Preheat oven to 350°F. Spray 9-inch baking pan with nonstick cooking spray.
2. Combine flour, brown sugar, oats, baking soda and salt in large bowl; mix well. Add butter and vanilla; mix with hands or stir with spatula until mixture is well blended and clumpy. Press 3 cups dough (loosely packed) into bottom of prepared pan. Cover and refrigerate remaining dough until ready to use. Bake crust 13 minutes.
3. Remove pan from oven. Drizzle with caramel sauce; sprinkle with chocolate chips. Drop chunks of reserved dough (1- to 2-inch pieces) evenly over chocolate chips.
4. Bake 15 minutes or until lightly browned. Cool completely in pan on wire rack.

Chocolate Cereal Bars

MAKES 2 TO 3 DOZEN BARS

- 6 cups crisp rice cereal
- 1 jar (7 ounces) marshmallow creme
- 1 cup semisweet chocolate chips
- 2 tablespoons butter
- 1 teaspoon vanilla

1. Spray 13×9-inch baking pan with nonstick cooking spray. Place cereal in large bowl.
2. Combine marshmallow creme, chocolate chips and butter in medium saucepan; heat over medium heat until mixture is melted and smooth, stirring occasionally. Remove from heat; stir in vanilla.
3. Pour chocolate mixture over cereal; stir until blended. Press evenly into prepared pan. Cool completely before cutting into bars.

Brownie Fixation

MAKES 9 SERVINGS

- ¾ cup (1½ sticks) butter, cut into pieces
- 4 ounces unsweetened chocolate, chopped
- 1¾ cups sugar
- 4 eggs
- 1 teaspoon vanilla
- ¾ cup all-purpose flour
- ½ teaspoon salt
- Hot fudge sauce
- Caramel ice cream topping
- Vanilla ice cream
- ¾ cup chopped pecans

1. Preheat oven to 350°F. Line 8-inch square baking pan with parchment paper or spray with nonstick cooking spray.
2. Combine butter and chocolate in medium saucepan; heat over low heat until melted, stirring frequently. Remove from heat; stir in sugar until well blended. Add eggs, one at a time, beating well after each addition. Stir in vanilla. Add flour and salt; stir just until blended. Spread batter in prepared pan.
3. Bake 20 to 23 minutes or until toothpick inserted into center comes out with fudgy crumbs. Cool in pan on wire rack 15 minutes.
4. Heat hot fudge sauce and caramel topping according to package directions. Cut brownie into nine squares.
5. For each serving, place one warm brownie on serving plate; drizzle with hot fudge sauce. Top with ice cream, caramel topping and pecans. Serve immediately.

Chocolate Almond Crispy Treats

MAKES 2 TO 3 DOZEN BARS

- **6 cups crisp brown rice cereal**
- **1½ cups sliced almonds, toasted***
- **1 cup light corn syrup**
- **⅓ cup almond butter**
- **¼ cup packed brown sugar**
- **3 tablespoons unsweetened cocoa powder**
- **¼ teaspoon salt**
- **1 cup semisweet chocolate chips**

To toast almonds, cook in large skillet over medium heat 2 to 3 minutes or until lightly browned, stirring frequently.

1. Line 13×9-inch baking pan with parchment paper; spray with nonstick cooking spray.
2. Combine cereal and almonds in large bowl; mix well. Combine corn syrup, almond butter, brown sugar, cocoa and salt in large saucepan; cook and stir over medium heat 5 minutes or until mixture is smooth and just begins to bubble across surface.
3. Remove from heat; immediately stir in cereal mixture until blended. Gently fold in chocolate chips.
4. Press mixture firmly into prepared pan. Let stand 1 hour or until set.

Celebration Brownies

MAKES 2 TO 3 DOZEN BROWNIES

- **1 cup (2 sticks) butter**
- **8 ounces semisweet chocolate, coarsely chopped**
- **1 cup sugar**
- **4 eggs**
- **1 teaspoon vanilla**
- **1 teaspoon salt**
- **1¼ cups all-purpose flour**
- **2 cups dark or semisweet chocolate chips, divided**
- **¼ cup whipping cream**
- **1 container (about 2 ounces) rainbow nonpareils**

1. Preheat oven to 350°F. Spray 13×9-inch baking pan with nonstick cooking spray or line with parchment paper.
2. Combine butter and chocolate in large saucepan; heat over low heat until melted, stirring frequently.
3. Remove from heat; stir in sugar until blended. Add eggs, one at a time, beating well after each addition. Stir in vanilla and salt. Add flour and 1 cup chocolate chips; stir just until blended. Spread batter evenly in prepared pan.
4. Bake 22 to 25 minutes or until center is set and toothpick inserted into center comes out with fudgy crumbs. Cool completely in pan on wire rack.
5. Heat cream in small saucepan over medium-low heat until bubbles appear around edge of pan. Remove from heat; add remaining 1 cup chocolate chips. Let stand 1 minute; whisk until smooth and well blended. Spread evenly over brownies; top with nonpareils.

Chocolate Chip Shortbread

MAKES 12 TO 16 BARS

- **½ cup (1 stick) butter, softened**
- **½ cup granulated sugar**
- **2 tablespoons packed brown sugar**
- **1 teaspoon vanilla**
- **1 cup all-purpose flour**
- **½ teaspoon salt**
- **½ cup plus 2 tablespoons mini semisweet chocolate chips, divided**

1. Preheat oven to 350°F.
2. Beat butter, granulated sugar and brown sugar in large bowl with electric mixer at medium speed about 3 minutes or until light and fluffy. Beat in vanilla. Add flour and salt; beat at low speed until combined. Stir in ½ cup chocolate chips.
3. Press dough evenly into ungreased 8- or 9-inch square baking pan. Sprinkle with remaining 2 tablespoons chocolate chips; press lightly into dough.
4. Bake 15 to 17 minutes or until edges are golden brown. Cool completely in pan on wire rack.

Variation

For shortbread wedges, press dough into two 8-inch round baking pans. Bake 12 to 15 minutes or until edges are golden brown and centers are set. Cool completely in pan on wire rack; cut each into eight wedges.

Pumpkin Swirl Brownies

MAKES 12 TO 16 BROWNIES

Pumpkin Swirl

- **4 ounces cream cheese, softened**
- **½ cup canned pumpkin**
- **1 egg**
- **3 tablespoons sugar**
- **¾ teaspoon pumpkin pie spice**
- **Pinch of salt**

Brownies

- **½ cup (1 stick) butter**
- **6 ounces semisweet chocolate, chopped**
- **1 cup sugar**
- **3 eggs**
- **1 teaspoon vanilla**
- **¾ cup all-purpose flour**
- **2 tablespoons unsweetened cocoa powder**
- **½ teaspoon salt**

1. Preheat oven to 350°F. Spray 8-inch square baking pan with nonstick cooking spray or line with parchment paper.
2. For swirl, combine cream cheese, pumpkin, 1 egg, 3 tablespoons sugar, pumpkin pie spice and pinch of salt in medium bowl; beat until smooth.
3. For brownies, combine butter and chocolate in medium saucepan; heat over low heat until melted, stirring frequently.
4. Remove from heat; stir in 1 cup sugar until blended. Add 3 eggs, one at a time, beating well after each addition. Stir in vanilla. Add flour, cocoa and ½ teaspoon salt; stir until blended. Reserve ⅓ cup brownie batter in small bowl; spread remaining batter in prepared pan.
5. Spread pumpkin mixture evenly over brownie batter. Drop reserved brownie batter by teaspoonfuls over pumpkin layer; draw tip of knife through top of both batters to marbleize. (If reserved brownie batter has become very thick upon standing, microwave on LOW (30%) 20 to 30 seconds or until loosened, stirring at 10-second intervals.)
6. Bake 28 to 30 minutes or just until center is set and edges begin to pull away from sides of pan. (Toothpick will come out with fudgy crumbs.) Cool completely in pan on wire rack.

Double Chocolate Dream Bars

MAKES 2 TO 3 DOZEN BARS

- **2¼ cups all-purpose flour, divided**
- **1 cup (2 sticks) butter, softened**
- **¾ cup powdered sugar, plus additional for garnish**
- **⅓ cup unsweetened cocoa powder**
- **½ teaspoon salt**
- **2 cups granulated sugar**
- **4 eggs**
- **4 ounces unsweetened chocolate, melted**

1. Preheat oven to 350°F. Line 13×9-inch baking pan with parchment paper.
2. Beat 2 cups flour, butter, ¾ cup powdered sugar, cocoa and salt in large bowl with electric mixer at low speed until blended. Beat at medium speed until well blended and stiff dough forms. Press firmly into prepared pan.
3. Bake crust 15 to 20 minutes or just until set. *Do not overbake.*
4. Meanwhile, combine remaining ¼ cup flour and granulated sugar in large bowl. Add eggs and melted chocolate; beat with electric mixer at medium-high speed until well blended. Pour over crust.
5. Bake 25 minutes or until center is firm to the touch. Cool completely in pan on wire rack. Sprinkle with additional powdered sugar, if desired.

Frosted Cocoa Brownies

MAKES ABOUT 2½ DOZEN BROWNIES

- 2 cups all-purpose flour
- 2 cups granulated sugar
- ½ teaspoon salt
- ½ cup buttermilk
- 2 eggs, lightly beaten
- 1 teaspoon baking soda
- 1 teaspoon vanilla
- 1 cup (2 sticks) butter
- 1 cup hot coffee
- ¼ cup unsweetened cocoa powder
- Cocoa Frosting (recipe follows)

1. Preheat oven to 400°F. Spray 17½×11-inch jelly-roll pan with nonstick cooking spray.
2. Combine flour, granulated sugar and salt in large bowl; mix well. Whisk buttermilk, eggs, baking soda and 1 teaspoon vanilla in medium bowl until well blended.
3. Combine 1 cup butter, coffee and ¼ cup cocoa in medium saucepan; bring to a simmer over medium heat until butter is melted and mixture is smooth, stirring constantly. Add to flour mixture; stir until blended. Stir in buttermilk mixture until well blended. Pour batter into prepared pan.
4. Bake 20 minutes or until center springs back when touched. Meanwhile, prepare Cocoa Frosting.
5. Remove brownies from oven; immediately pour warm frosting over hot brownies, spreading evenly. Cool in pan on wire rack.

Cocoa Frosting

- ½ cup (1 stick) butter
- 2 tablespoons unsweetened cocoa powder
- ¼ cup milk
- 3½ cups powdered sugar
- 1 teaspoon vanilla

Combine ½ cup butter, 2 tablespoons cocoa and milk in large saucepan; bring to a boil over medium heat. Remove from heat; beat in powdered sugar and 1 teaspoon vanilla until frosting is smooth and creamy.

Chocolate Chunk Oat Bars

MAKES 12 TO 16 BARS

- 1 cup all-purpose flour
- ½ teaspoon baking soda
- ½ teaspoon salt
- 1 cup packed brown sugar
- ½ cup (1 stick) butter, softened
- 1 egg
- 1 tablespoon water
- 1 teaspoon vanilla
- 1½ cups old-fashioned oats
- 2 cups semisweet chocolate chunks, divided

1. Preheat oven to 375°F. Spray 9-inch square baking pan with nonstick cooking spray.
2. Combine flour, baking soda and salt in small bowl; mix well. Beat brown sugar and butter in large bowl with electric mixer at medium-high speed about 3 minutes or until creamy. Add egg, water and vanilla; beat until well blended. Stir in flour mixture and oats; mix well. Stir in 1½ cups chocolate chunks.
3. Spread dough evenly in prepared pan; sprinkle with remaining ½ cup chocolate chunks.
4. Bake about 30 minutes or just until center feels firm. Cool completely in pan on wire rack.

Nutty Chocolate Crumble Bars

MAKES 2 TO 3 DOZEN BARS

- 1 cup all-purpose flour
- 1 cup old-fashioned oats
- ¾ cup packed brown sugar
- ½ cup (1 stick) butter, softened
- 1 can (14 ounces) sweetened condensed milk
- 1 cup chopped walnuts or pecans
- 1 cup semisweet chocolate chips

1. Preheat oven to 350°F. Combine flour, oats, brown sugar and butter in large bowl; stir until mixture is crumbly.
2. Reserve ½ cup oat mixture for topping. Press remaining mixture into bottom of ungreased 13×9-inch baking pan.
3. Bake 10 minutes. Remove pan from oven; pour condensed milk evenly over crust. Sprinkle with walnuts and chocolate chips. Top with reserved oat mixture; press down firmly.
4. Bake 25 minutes or until top is lightly browned. Cool completely in pan on wire rack.

Marbled Cookie Brownie

MAKES 12 TO 16 BROWNIES

- 1 cup plus 1 tablespoon all-purpose flour
- ½ teaspoon baking soda
- ½ teaspoon salt
- ½ cup (1 stick) butter, softened
- ½ cup packed brown sugar
- ¼ cup granulated sugar
- 1 egg
- ½ teaspoon vanilla
- 1 cup milk chocolate chips
- 1 package (18 to 19 ounces) brownie mix, plus ingredients to prepare mix

1. Preheat oven to 350°F. Line 9-inch square baking pan with parchment paper; spray paper with nonstick cooking spray.
2. For cookies, combine flour, baking soda and salt in small bowl; mix well. Beat butter, brown sugar and granulated sugar in large bowl with electric mixer at medium speed about 3 minutes or until light and fluffy, scraping down side of bowl twice. Add egg; beat until well blended. Beat in vanilla. Gradually add flour mixture; beat at low speed just until blended. Stir in chocolate chips. Cover and refrigerate cookie dough while preparing brownies.
3. Prepare brownie mix according to package directions. Spread batter in prepared pan; smooth top. Scoop out eight 1½-tablespoon balls of cookie dough; roll into smooth, round balls. (Reserve remaining cookie dough for another use.) Scatter cookie dough balls over brownie batter; press down gently to push cookie dough into brownie batter.
4. Bake 25 minutes, then cover loosely with foil to prevent cookies from becoming too brown. Bake 13 minutes or until brownies are firm, edges begin to come away from side of pan and toothpick inserted into center comes out clean. Cool in pan on wire rack 10 minutes. Serve warm or at room temperature.

Cocoa Bottom Banana Pecan Bars

MAKES 2 TO 3 DOZEN BARS

- 1½ cups all-purpose flour
- 1 teaspoon baking powder
- 1 teaspoon baking soda
- ½ teaspoon salt
- 1 cup sugar
- ½ cup (1 stick) butter, softened
- 5 ripe bananas, mashed
- 1 egg
- 1 teaspoon vanilla
- ½ cup chopped pecans
- ¼ cup unsweetened cocoa powder

1. Preheat oven to 350°F. Spray 13×9-inch baking pan with nonstick cooking spray.
2. Combine flour, baking powder, baking soda and salt in medium bowl; mix well. Beat sugar and butter in large bowl with electric mixer at medium speed about 3 minutes or until creamy. Add bananas, egg and vanilla; beat until well blended. Add flour mixture; beat at low speed just until blended. Stir in pecans.
3. Remove half of batter to medium bowl; stir in cocoa until blended. Spread chocolate batter in prepared pan. Top with plain batter; swirl with knife to marbleize.
4. Bake 30 to 35 minutes or until edges are lightly browned. Cool completely in pan on wire rack.

Chocolate Peanut Butter Cereal Treats

MAKES 2 TO 3 DOZEN BARS

- ½ cup peanut butter
- ⅓ cup semisweet chocolate chips
- 1 tablespoon butter
- 5 cups mini marshmallows
- 6 cups crisp rice cereal
- 1 package (4 ounces) candy-coated peanut butter pieces

1. Line 13×9-inch baking pan with foil; spray with nonstick cooking spray.
2. Combine peanut butter, chocolate chips and butter in large saucepan; heat over low heat until mixture is melted and smooth, stirring frequently.
3. Add marshmallows; cook and stir 5 minutes or until melted and smooth. Remove from heat; stir in cereal and peanut butter pieces.
4. Press evenly into prepared pan. Cool completely before cutting into bars.

Double Chocolate Pecan Brownies

MAKES 12 TO 16 BROWNIES

- 1 cup plus 2 tablespoons all-purpose flour
- ¾ cup unsweetened cocoa powder
- ½ teaspoon baking powder
- ¼ teaspoon salt
- 1¼ cups sugar
- ½ cup (1 stick) butter, softened
- 2 eggs
- 1 teaspoon vanilla
- ½ cup semisweet chocolate chips
- ½ cup chopped pecans

1. Preheat oven to 350°F. Line 8-inch square baking pan with foil, extending foil over two sides of pan. Spray foil with nonstick cooking spray.
2. Combine flour, cocoa, baking powder and salt in medium bowl; mix well. Beat sugar and butter in large bowl with electric mixer at medium speed 2 to 3 minutes or until creamy. Add eggs, one at a time, beating well after each addition. Beat in vanilla. Gradually add flour mixture; beat at low speed just until blended. Spread batter in prepared pan (batter will be very thick). Sprinkle with chocolate chips and pecans.
3. Bake about 30 minutes or until toothpick inserted into center comes out almost clean. Cool in pan 5 minutes; use foil to remove brownies to wire rack to cool completely.

Cakes and Cheesecakes

Death by Chocolate Poke Cake

MAKES 12 TO 16 SERVINGS

- 1 package (about 15 ounces) dark chocolate cake mix, plus ingredients to prepare mix
- 1 cup semisweet chocolate chips
- 1 package (4-serving size) chocolate instant pudding and pie filling mix, plus ingredients to prepare mix
- 1 cup white chocolate chips

1. Prepare cake mix according to package directions; stir in chocolate chips. Bake cake according to package directions for 13×9-inch pan. Cool completely in pan on wire rack.
2. Poke holes in cake at ½-inch intervals with wooden skewer. Prepare pudding according to package directions.
3. Pour pudding evenly over cake; top with white chocolate chips. Refrigerate 2 to 3 hours or until firm.

Chocolate Peppermint Cheesecake

MAKES 12 SERVINGS

- Chocolate Crumb Crust (recipe follows)
- 1 package (12 ounces) semisweet chocolate chips
- ¾ cup whipping cream
- 3 packages (8 ounces each) cream cheese, softened
- ¾ cup packed brown sugar
- 3 eggs
- ¼ cup unsweetened cocoa powder
- 1 teaspoon mint extract
- ½ teaspoon vanilla
- Whipped cream (optional)
- Crushed peppermint candy (optional)

1. Preheat oven to 325°F. Prepare Chocolate Crumb Crust.
2. Combine chocolate chips and cream in medium saucepan; heat over low heat until chocolate is melted and mixture is smooth, stirring frequently. Set aside to cool slightly.
3. Beat cream cheese in large bowl with electric mixer at medium speed 3 to 4 minutes or until light and fluffy. Add brown sugar; beat until light and fluffy. Add eggs, one at a time, beating at low speed until well blended. Beat in cocoa, mint extract and vanilla. Beat in melted chocolate mixture until blended, scraping side of bowl frequently. Pour filling into prepared crust.
4. Bake 45 to 50 minutes or until center is just set. Remove to wire rack; carefully loosen edge of cheesecake with knife. Cool completely on wire rack. Refrigerate several hours or overnight.
5. Remove side of pan. Top with whipped cream and candy, if desired.

Chocolate Crumb Crust

Preheat oven to 325°F. Combine 1 cup chocolate wafer crumbs and 3 tablespoons melted butter in small bowl until well blended. Press into bottom of 9-inch springform pan. Bake 10 minutes. Cool on wire rack while preparing filling.

Classic Chocolate Buttermilk Birthday Cake

MAKES 12 SERVINGS

- 2 cups all-purpose flour
- 3¼ cups sugar, divided
- ⅔ cup unsweetened cocoa powder
- 2 teaspoons baking soda
- 1½ teaspoons baking powder
- ¾ teaspoon salt
- 1¾ cups buttermilk
- ½ cup vegetable oil
- 2 eggs
- 2 teaspoons vanilla, divided
- 6 ounces unsweetened chocolate, chopped
- ½ cup (1 stick) butter
- 1 cup whipping cream

1. Preheat oven to 350°F. Line bottoms of two 9-inch round cake pans with parchment paper; spray pans and paper with nonstick cooking spray.
2. Combine flour, 1¾ cups sugar, cocoa, baking soda, baking powder and salt in large bowl; mix well. Whisk buttermilk, oil, eggs and 1 teaspoon vanilla in medium bowl until well blended. Add to flour mixture; stir until well blended. Pour batter into prepared pans.
3. Bake 22 to 24 minutes or until toothpick inserted into centers comes out clean. Cool in pans 10 minutes; remove to wire racks to cool completely.
4. Combine chocolate and butter in medium bowl. Combine remaining 1½ cups sugar and cream in small saucepan; heat over medium-high heat until sugar is dissolved, stirring frequently. When cream begins to bubble, reduce heat to low and simmer 5 minutes. Pour over chocolate and butter; stir until smooth. Stir in remaining 1 teaspoon vanilla. Refrigerate until frosting is cool and thickened, stirring occasionally.
5. Place one cake layer on serving plate; spread with 1 cup frosting. Top with second cake layer; frost top and side of cake with remaining frosting. Refrigerate at least 1 hour before slicing.

Tip

For neat cake slices, run a long sharp knife (not serrated) under hot water to warm it and wipe dry immediately before slicing. Wipe off the knife with paper towels after every cut and rewarm it under hot water as needed.

Bittersweet Chocolate Raspberry Cupcakes

MAKES 20 CUPCAKES

- 1½ cups all-purpose flour
- 1 teaspoon baking soda
- 1 teaspoon baking powder
- ½ teaspoon salt
- ¾ cup hot coffee
- ¾ cup unsweetened cocoa powder
- 8 ounces bittersweet chocolate, chopped, divided
- 1¼ cups sugar
- 2 eggs
- ⅓ cup vegetable oil
- 1 teaspoon vanilla
- ¾ cup buttermilk
- 2 pints fresh raspberries, divided
- ½ cup whipping cream

1. Preheat oven to 350°F. Line 20 standard (2½-inch) muffin cups with paper baking cups.
2. Combine flour, baking soda, baking powder and salt in small bowl; mix well. Whisk coffee, cocoa and 2 ounces chocolate in large bowl until chocolate is melted and mixture is smooth. Whisk in sugar, eggs, oil and vanilla until well blended. Add flour mixture alternately with buttermilk, stirring until blended after each addition. Spoon batter evenly into prepared muffin cups; place three raspberries in each cup.
3. Bake 22 minutes or until toothpick inserted into centers comes out clean. Cool in pans 5 minutes; remove to wire racks to cool completely.
4. Meanwhile, place remaining 6 ounces chocolate in medium bowl. Heat cream to a simmer in small saucepan over medium heat or in microwave. Pour cream over chocolate; let stand 2 minutes. Whisk until well blended and smooth.
5. Dip tops of cupcakes in chocolate mixture; return to wire racks. Top with raspberries. Let stand until set.

Chocolate Peanut Butter Oatmeal Snack Cake

MAKES 12 TO 16 SERVINGS

- 1¼ cups boiling water
- 1 cup old-fashioned oats
- 1 cup granulated sugar
- 1 cup packed brown sugar
- ½ cup (1 stick) butter, softened
- 2 eggs, beaten
- 1 teaspoon vanilla
- 1¾ cups all-purpose flour
- ¼ cup unsweetened cocoa powder
- 1 teaspoon baking soda
- 2 cups semisweet chocolate chips, divided
- 1 cup peanut butter chips

1. Preheat oven to 350°F. Spray 13×9-inch baking pan with nonstick cooking spray.
2. Stir boiling water into oats in large bowl; let stand 10 minutes. Stir until water is absorbed.
3. Add granulated sugar, brown sugar and butter to oat mixture; beat with electric mixer at low speed 1 minute or until well blended. Add eggs and vanilla; beat until blended.
4. Combine flour, cocoa and baking soda in medium bowl; mix well. Gradually add to oat mixture; beat at low speed until well blended. Stir in 1 cup chocolate chips. Pour batter into prepared pan; sprinkle with remaining 1 cup chocolate chips and peanut butter chips.
5. Bake 40 minutes or until toothpick inserted into center comes out clean. Cool completely in pan on wire rack.

Chocolate Marble Cake

MAKES 12 SERVINGS

- 2½ cups all-purpose flour
- 2 cups sugar, divided
- 2 teaspoons baking powder
- 1¼ teaspoons baking soda, divided
- 1 teaspoon salt
- 1⅔ cups buttermilk
- ¾ cup (1½ sticks) butter, softened, cut into small pieces
- 3 eggs, beaten
- 1 tablespoon vanilla
- ⅓ cup unsweetened cocoa powder
- ¼ cup water
- ½ teaspoon espresso powder
- Chocolate Glaze (recipe follows)

1. Preheat oven to 375°F. Grease and flour 12-cup (10-inch) bundt pan.
2. Combine flour, 1⅔ cups sugar, baking powder, 1 teaspoon baking soda and salt in large bowl; mix well. Add buttermilk, butter, eggs and vanilla; beat with electric mixer at low speed 1 minute. Beat at medium speed 2 to 3 minutes or until well blended. Remove ¾ cup batter to medium bowl.
3. Combine remaining ⅓ cup sugar, ¼ teaspoon baking soda, cocoa, water and espresso powder in small bowl; stir until blended and smooth. Add to ¾ cup reserved batter; mix well. Spoon vanilla batter into prepared pan; drop spoonfuls of chocolate batter over vanilla batter. Swirl with knife or skewer to marbleize.
4. Bake 40 to 45 minutes or until toothpick inserted near center comes out clean. Cool in pan 15 minutes; invert onto wire rack to cool completely.
5. Prepare Chocolate Glaze; drizzle over cake. Let stand until set.

Chocolate Glaze

Combine ¼ cup unsweetened cocoa powder, 3 tablespoons light corn syrup and 1½ tablespoons water in small saucepan; cook and stir over medium heat until thickened. Remove from heat; stir in 1 cup powdered sugar and ¼ teaspoon vanilla until smooth.

Rich Mocha Cheesecake

MAKES 12 SERVINGS

- 1 package or pouch (about 10 ounces) fudge brownie mix
- ¼ cup vegetable or canola oil
- ¼ cup water
- 4 eggs, divided
- 1 cup semisweet chocolate chips
- ⅓ cup whipping cream
- 1½ tablespoons instant coffee granules
- 3 packages (8 ounces each) cream cheese, softened
- ¼ cup (½ stick) butter, softened
- 1 cup sugar
- 1 teaspoon vanilla
- 1 jar (10 ounces) raspberry fruit spread
- Whipped cream and fresh raspberries (optional)

1. Preheat oven to 350°F. Spray 9-inch springform pan with nonstick cooking spray.
2. Stir brownie mix, oil, water and 1 egg in medium bowl until well blended. Pour batter into prepared pan. Bake 20 minutes or until toothpick inserted 2 inches from edge comes out clean. Cool in pan on wire rack.
3. Combine chocolate chips, cream and coffee granules in small saucepan; heat over medium-low heat until chocolate is melted and mixture is smooth, stirring frequently. Remove from heat; set aside 10 to 15 minutes to cool.
4. Beat cream cheese and butter in large bowl with electric mixer at medium-high speed until smooth. Add sugar; beat about 3 minutes or until light and fluffy. Add remaining 3 eggs, one at a time, beating well after each addition. Add vanilla and melted chocolate mixture; beat at low speed just until blended.
5. Remove lid from fruit spread. Microwave on HIGH 30 seconds; stir until melted and smooth. (Jar may be very hot.) Pour melted fruit spread evenly over baked crust; pour cheesecake filling over fruit spread.
6. Bake 40 minutes or until edge is set but center is still moist. Cool completely in pan on wire rack. Cover and refrigerate 24 hours. Let stand at room temperature 30 minutes before serving. Garnish with whipped cream and raspberries.

Fudgy Cola Cake

MAKES 12 TO 16 SERVINGS

Cake

- 2 cups granulated sugar
- 2 cups all-purpose flour
- 1 teaspoon baking soda
- ½ teaspoon salt
- ½ cup buttermilk
- 2 eggs
- 1 teaspoon vanilla extract
- 1 cup cola
- ½ cup (1 stick) butter
- ½ cup vegetable oil
- ¼ cup unsweetened Dutch process or regular cocoa powder

Icing

- ½ cup (1 stick) butter
- ½ cup cola
- ¼ cup unsweetened Dutch process or regular cocoa powder
- 4 cups powdered sugar, sifted

1. Preheat oven to 350°F. Spray 13×9-inch baking pan with nonstick cooking spray.
2. For cake, sift granulated sugar, flour, baking soda and salt into large bowl. Whisk buttermilk, eggs and vanilla in measuring cup until blended. (Mixture may look curdled.)
3. Combine 1 cup cola, ½ cup butter, oil and ¼ cup cocoa in medium saucepan; bring to a boil over medium heat, stirring frequently. Pour over flour mixture; stir until blended. Stir in buttermilk mixture until blended. Pour batter into prepared pan.
4. Bake 30 to 35 minutes or until toothpick inserted into center comes out clean. Meanwhile, prepare icing.
5. For icing, combine ½ cup butter, ½ cup cola and ¼ cup cocoa in medium saucepan; bring to a boil over medium heat, stirring frequently. Remove from heat; whisk in powdered sugar until well blended and smooth. Pour icing evenly over warm cake. Cool to room temperature in pan on wire rack.

Warm Chocolate Soufflé Cakes

MAKES 4 SERVINGS

- **6 tablespoons (¾ stick) butter**
- **4 ounces semisweet chocolate, chopped**
- **½ cup granulated sugar**
- **1½ tablespoons cornstarch**
- **⅛ teaspoon salt**
- **2 eggs**
- **2 egg yolks**
- **Raspberry Sauce (optional, recipe follows)**
- **Powdered sugar**

1. Spray four 6-ounce ramekins with nonstick cooking spray. Place on small baking sheet.
2. Combine butter and chocolate in small saucepan; heat over low heat until melted, stirring frequently.
3. Combine granulated sugar, cornstarch and salt in medium bowl; mix well. Gradually add chocolate mixture; whisk until well blended.
4. Whisk eggs and egg yolks in small bowl. Add to chocolate mixture; whisk just until blended. Divide batter evenly among prepared ramekins; cover and refrigerate overnight. Prepare Raspberry Sauce, if desired.
5. Preheat oven to 375°F. Bake cakes 18 to 20 minutes or just until barely set (batter does not jiggle or look shiny). Sprinkle with powdered sugar; serve with Raspberry Sauce.

Raspberry Sauce

Combine 1 (12-ounce) package thawed frozen raspberries and ¼ cup granulated sugar in food processor or blender; process until smooth. Press through fine-mesh sieve to remove seeds.

Chocolate Storm

MAKES 9 TO 12 SERVINGS

- 12 ounces semisweet chocolate, chopped
- 12 ounces bittersweet chocolate, chopped
- ¾ cup (1½ sticks) butter, cut into pieces
- 5 eggs
- ⅔ cup granulated sugar
- 2 teaspoons vanilla
- ½ teaspoon salt
- 1¼ cups chopped pecans
- 2 cups cold whipping cream
- ¼ cup powdered sugar
- 3 pints vanilla ice cream
- 1½ cups hot fudge topping, heated
- Whipped cream and chocolate curls (optional)

1. Preheat oven to 325°F. Spray 9-inch square baking pan with nonstick cooking spray.
2. Combine semisweet chocolate, bittersweet chocolate and butter in medium microwavable bowl. Microwave on HIGH 1 minute; stir and repeat. Microwave 30 seconds; stir until chocolate is melted and mixture is smooth.
3. Beat eggs, granulated sugar, vanilla and salt in large bowl with electric mixer at medium speed 1 minute. Beat at high speed 1 minute. Add half of chocolate mixture; beat at low speed until blended. Beat in remaining chocolate mixture until blended. Stir in pecans. Pour batter into prepared pan; smooth top.
4. Bake about 45 minutes or until center begins to firm. Cool in pan on wire rack.
5. When ready to serve, beat cream and powdered sugar in medium bowl with electric mixer at medium-high speed until stiff peaks form.
6. Cut cake into nine squares. If desired, heat individual cake squares in microwave on HIGH 30 seconds. Top warm cake with ice cream, hot fudge, whipped cream and chocolate curls, if desired.

Devil's Food Sheet Cake

MAKES 12 TO 16 SERVINGS

Cake

- 1½ cups granulated sugar
- 1½ cups all-purpose flour
- ¾ cup unsweetened cocoa powder
- ½ cup packed brown sugar
- 1½ teaspoons baking soda
- 1½ teaspoons baking powder
- 1 teaspoon salt
- 1 cup buttermilk or milk
- 2 eggs
- ½ cup vegetable oil
- 1 teaspoon vanilla
- 1 cup boiling water
- 2 teaspoons instant coffee granules or instant espresso powder

Frosting

- 1 can (15 ounces) sweet potato purée
- Pinch of salt
- 1 package (10 ounces) bittersweet or semisweet chocolate chips
- ½ teaspoon vanilla
- Colored decors (optional)

1. Preheat oven to 350°F. Spray 13×9-inch baking pan with nonstick cooking spray or line with parchment paper.
2. For cake, combine granulated sugar, flour, cocoa, brown sugar, baking soda, baking powder and 1 teaspoon salt in large bowl of electric mixer; beat at low speed to blend. Add buttermilk, eggs, oil and 1 teaspoon vanilla; beat at medium speed 2 minutes.
3. Stir boiling water into coffee granules in small bowl or measuring cup until well blended. Add to chocolate mixture; stir until blended. (Batter will be thin.) Pour batter into prepared pan.
4. Bake about 30 minutes or until top appears dry and toothpick inserted into center comes out clean. Cool completely in pan on wire rack.
5. For frosting, combine sweet potato purée and pinch of salt in large saucepan; bring to a simmer over medium heat, stirring frequently. Remove from heat; stir in chocolate chips and ½ teaspoon vanilla until chocolate is melted and mixture is smooth. Let stand until frosting is thickened and cooled to room temperature, stirring occasionally.
6. Spread frosting over cake; sprinkle with decors, if desired.

Note

You can substitute a more traditional chocolate frosting (on pages 98 or 120) for the sweet potato chocolate frosting.

Double Peanut Butter Milk Chocolate Cupcakes

MAKES 42 MINI CUPCAKES

- 1 package (12 ounces) milk chocolate chips, divided
- ¼ cup (½ stick) butter
- 1½ cups all-purpose flour
- ½ cup sugar
- 1 teaspoon baking powder
- ½ teaspoon salt
- ¾ cup buttermilk*
- 2 eggs
- 1 teaspoon vanilla
- 42 mini chocolate peanut butter cups (¾ inch in diameter, not individually wrapped)
- ¼ cup whipping cream
- ¼ cup peanut butter

**Or substitute 2¼ teaspoons vinegar or lemon juice plus enough milk to equal ¾ cup. Stir; let stand 5 minutes.*

1. Preheat oven to 350°F. Line 42 mini (1¾-inch) muffin cups with paper baking cups.
2. Combine 1 cup chocolate chips and butter in small microwavable bowl; microwave on HIGH 30 seconds. Stir; microwave at 10-second intervals until chocolate is melted. Stir until blended and smooth; set aside to cool slightly.
3. Combine flour, sugar, baking powder and salt in large bowl; mix well. Whisk buttermilk, eggs and vanilla in small bowl until blended. Add buttermilk mixture and chocolate mixture to flour mixture; stir until blended. Pour batter into prepared muffin cups, filling half. Place one peanut butter cup in each muffin cup; top with remaining batter. (Cups will be almost full.)
4. Bake 12 minutes or until toothpick inserted near centers comes out clean. Cool cupcakes in pans 5 minutes; remove to wire racks to cool.
5. Place remaining chocolate chips in medium bowl. Heat cream to a simmer in small saucepan over medium heat; pour over chocolate chips. Let stand 5 minutes; stir until blended and smooth. Set ganache aside about 20 minutes to thicken.
6. Place peanut butter in small microwavable bowl; microwave on MEDIUM (50%) about 15 seconds or just until softened. Dip tops of cupcakes in ganache; return to wire racks. Use toothpick to add streaks of softened peanut butter to ganache topping. Let stand until set.

Flourless Chocolate Cake

MAKES 8 TO 10 SERVINGS

- **16 ounces semisweet chocolate, chopped**
- **½ cup (1 stick) butter**
- **4 eggs, at room temperature, separated**
- **¼ cup sugar**
- **2 tablespoons water**
- **½ teaspoon vanilla**
- **½ cup seedless raspberry jam (optional)**
- **Whipped cream (optional)**

1. Preheat oven to 350°F. Spray 9-inch springform pan with nonstick cooking spray.
2. Combine chocolate and butter in medium saucepan; heat over low heat until melted, stirring frequently. Remove from heat; whisk in egg yolks, sugar, water and vanilla until well blended.
3. Beat egg whites in large bowl with electric mixer at medium speed. Gradually increase speed to high; beat until stiff peaks form. Fold in one third of chocolate mixture at a time until no white streaks remain. Pour batter into prepared pan; smooth top.
4. Bake 22 to 25 minutes or until center is set. Cool in pan on wire rack 30 minutes.
5. If desired, place raspberry jam in small microwavable bowl; microwave on HIGH 30 seconds or until melted. Drizzle cake with jam; top with whipped cream, if desired.

Chocolate Espresso Cake

MAKES 12 SERVINGS

- 2 cups cake flour
- 1½ teaspoons baking soda
- ½ teaspoon salt
- ½ cup (1 stick) butter, softened
- 1 cup granulated sugar
- 1 cup packed brown sugar
- 3 eggs
- 4 ounces unsweetened chocolate, melted
- ¾ cup sour cream
- 1 teaspoon vanilla
- 1 cup brewed espresso*
- Creamy Chocolate Frosting (recipe follows)

**Use fresh brewed espresso, instant espresso powder prepared according to directions on jar or 1 tablespoon instant coffee granules dissolved in 1 cup hot water.*

1. Preheat oven to 350°F. Line bottoms of two 9-inch round cake pans with parchment paper; spray paper with nonstick cooking spray.

2. Combine flour, baking soda and salt in medium bowl; mix well. Beat butter, granulated sugar and brown sugar in large bowl with electric mixer at medium speed until light and fluffy. Add eggs, one at a time, beating well after each addition. Add melted chocolate, sour cream and vanilla; beat until blended. Add flour mixture alternately with espresso, beating until blended after each addition. Pour batter into prepared pans.

3. Bake 35 minutes or until toothpick inserted into center comes out clean. Cool in pans 10 minutes; iinvert onto wire racks to cool completely.

4. Prepare Creamy Chocolate Frosting. Place one cake layer on serving plate; spread with frosting. Top with second cake layer; frost top and side of cake.

Creamy Chocolate Frosting

- ½ cup (1 stick) butter, softened
- 4 cups powdered sugar
- 5 to 6 tablespoons brewed espresso, divided
- ½ cup (3 ounces) semisweet chocolate chips, melted
- 1 teaspoon vanilla
- Pinch of salt

Beat butter in large bowl with electric mixer at medium speed 2 to 3 minutes or until creamy. Gradually add powdered sugar and 4 tablespoons espresso; beat until smooth. Beat in melted chocolate, vanilla and salt. Add remaining espresso, 1 tablespoon at a time, until frosting reaches desired spreading consistency.

Chocolate Swirled Praline Cheesecake

MAKES 12 SERVINGS

Crust

- 1½ cups vanilla wafer crumbs
- ¼ cup powdered sugar
- ¼ cup (½ stick) butter, melted
- ½ cup finely chopped toasted pecans*

Filling

- 1¼ cups packed brown sugar
- 2 tablespoons all-purpose flour
- 3 packages (8 ounces each) cream cheese, softened
- 3 eggs, lightly beaten
- 1½ teaspoons vanilla
- 1 ounce unsweetened chocolate, melted
- 20 to 25 pecan halves (½ cup)
- Caramel ice cream topping

**To toast pecans, spread on ungreased baking sheet. Bake in preheated 350°F oven 6 to 8 minutes or until fragrant, stirring occasionally.*

1. Preheat oven to 350°F.
2. For crust, combine wafer crumbs, powdered sugar, butter and chopped pecans in large bowl; mix well. Press mixture onto bottom and up side of ungreased 9-inch springform pan. Bake 10 to 15 minutes or until lightly browned.
3. Meanwhile, for filling, combine brown sugar and flour in small bowl; mix well. Beat cream cheese in large bowl with electric mixer at medium speed about 3 minutes or until fluffy. Gradually add brown sugar mixture; beat until well blended. Add eggs and vanilla; beat until blended.
4. Remove 1 cup filling to small bowl; stir in melted chocolate. Pour remaining plain filling into warm crust. Drop spoonfuls of chocolate filling over plain filling; run knife through fillings to marbleize. Arrange pecan halves around edge.
5. Bake 45 to 55 minutes or until center is just set. Loosen cake from side of pan; cool completely on wire rack. Refrigerate 2 hours or until ready to serve.
6. Remove side of pan. Drizzle with caramel topping.

Molten Chocolate Cakes

MAKES 8 SERVINGS

- 1 package (about 15 ounces) chocolate fudge cake mix
- 1½ cups water
- 3 eggs
- ½ cup canola or vegetable oil
- 4 ounces bittersweet chocolate, chopped
- 4 ounces semisweet chocolate, chopped
- ½ cup whipping cream
- ¼ cup (½ stick) butter, cut into small pieces
- 1 tablespoon light corn syrup
- ¼ teaspoon vanilla
- ⅛ teaspoon salt
- Caramel ice cream topping
- Vanilla ice cream

1. Preheat oven to 350°F. Spray eight jumbo (3½-inch) muffin cups with nonstick cooking spray.
2. Beat cake mix, water, eggs and oil in large bowl with electric mixer at low speed 30 seconds. Beat at medium speed 2 minutes. Pour ½ cup batter into each prepared muffin cup; discard remaining batter or reserve for another use. Bake 25 minutes or until toothpick inserted into centers comes out clean. Cool in pans 5 minutes; remove to wire racks to cool.
3. Meanwhile, combine bittersweet chocolate, semisweet chocolate, cream, butter, corn syrup, vanilla and salt in medium microwavable bowl; microwave on HIGH 30 seconds. Stir; microwave at additional 30-second intervals until chocolate begins to melt. Whisk until smooth. Reserve ½ cup chocolate mixture in small microwavable bowl for topping.
4. When cakes have cooled, cut off domed top of each cake with serrated knife. Invert cakes so wider part is on the bottom. Use 1½-inch biscuit cutter or small serrated knife to remove hole in top of each cake (narrow part) about 1 inch deep. Reserve cake from holes for serving.
5. Fill hole in each cake with 2 tablespoons chocolate mixture; top with reserved cake pieces. Microwave reserved ½ cup chocolate mixture on HIGH 20 seconds or until melted.
6. For each serving, drizzle caramel topping on microwavable plate. Arrange cake on plate; microwave on HIGH 30 seconds until chocolate filling is hot. Top with ice cream; drizzle with warm chocolate mixture.

Chocolate Pumpkin Cake with Broiled Coconut Pecan Frosting

MAKES 12 TO 16 SERVINGS

- 2 cups all-purpose flour
- 1 cup quick oats
- ⅔ cup unsweetened cocoa powder
- 1 tablespoon ground cinnamon
- 2 teaspoons baking powder
- 1 teaspoon baking soda
- 1 teaspoon salt
- ½ teaspoon ground cloves
- 2 cups granulated sugar
- 1½ cups (3 sticks) butter, softened
- 4 eggs
- 1 can (15 ounces) pure pumpkin
- 1 can (8 ounces) crushed pineapple
- 1 teaspoon almond extract
- 1 cup packed brown sugar
- ½ cup whole milk or half-and-half
- 1½ cups flaked coconut
- 1½ cups pecans, chopped

1. Preheat oven to 350°F. Grease and flour 13×9-inch baking pan.

2. Combine flour, oats, cocoa, cinnamon, baking powder, baking soda, salt and cloves in medium bowl; mix well. Beat granulated sugar and 1 cup butter in large bowl with electric mixer at medium-high speed about 3 minutes or until creamy. Add eggs, one at a time, beating well after each addition. Add pumpkin, pineapple and almond extract; beat until well blended. Gradually add flour mixture at low speed; beat just until blended. Spread batter in prepared pan.

3. Bake 40 to 45 minutes or until toothpick inserted into center comes out clean.

4. Preheat broiler. Melt remaining ½ cup butter in medium saucepan over low heat. Stir in brown sugar and milk until smooth. Stir in coconut and pecans. Spread frosting over warm cake.

5. Broil 3 to 4 inches from heat source 3 to 4 minutes or until frosting is golden brown and bubbling. Cool completely in pan on wire rack.

Chocolate Peanut Butter Pudding Cake

MAKES ABOUT 8 SERVINGS

- 1¼ cups granulated sugar, divided
- 1 cup all-purpose flour
- ½ cup unsweetened cocoa powder, divided
- 1 teaspoon baking powder
- 1 teaspoon baking soda
- ¼ teaspoon salt
- ½ cup sour cream
- ½ cup creamy peanut butter
- 3 tablespoons butter, melted
- 4 tablespoons hot water
- ¼ cup packed brown sugar
- 1½ cups boiling water
- Whipped cream (optional)

1. Preheat oven to 350°F. Spray 8-inch square baking dish with nonstick cooking spray.
2. Combine ¾ cup granulated sugar, flour, ¼ cup cocoa, baking powder, baking soda and salt in large bowl; mix well. Whisk sour cream, peanut butter and butter in medium bowl until well blended. Gradually whisk in 4 tablespoons hot water until smooth. Add to flour mixture, stir until well blended. (Batter will be thick.) Spread batter in prepared pan; smooth top into even layer.
3. Combine remaining ½ cup granulated sugar, ¼ cup cocoa and brown sugar in small bowl; mix well. Sprinkle evenly over batter. Pour boiling water over sugar layer (do not stir).
4. Bake about 35 minutes or until center is almost set. Let stand 10 minutes before serving. Serve in bowls or dessert dishes, spooning sauce from bottom of dish over cake. Top with whipped cream, if desired.

Pies and Tarts

French Silk Pie

MAKES 8 SERVINGS

- 1 (9-inch) deep-dish pie crust (frozen or refrigerated)
- 1⅓ cups granulated sugar
- ¾ cup (1½ sticks) butter, softened
- 4 ounces unsweetened chocolate, melted
- 1½ tablespoons unsweetened cocoa powder
- 1 teaspoon vanilla
- ⅛ teaspoon salt
- 4 pasteurized eggs*
- 1 cup whipping cream
- 2 tablespoons powdered sugar
- Chocolate curls (optional)

***The eggs in this recipe are not cooked, so use pasteurized eggs to ensure food safety.**

1. Bake pie crust according to package directions. Cool completely on wire rack.
2. Beat granulated sugar and butter in large bowl with electric mixer at medium speed about 3 minutes or until light and fluffy. Add melted chocolate, cocoa, vanilla and salt; beat until well blended. Add eggs, one at a time, beating 4 minutes after each addition and scraping down side of bowl occasionally.
3. Spread filling in cooled crust. Refrigerate at least 3 hours or overnight.
4. Beat cream and powdered sugar in medium bowl with electric mixer at high speed until soft peaks form. Pipe or spread whipped cream over chocolate layer; garnish with chocolate curls.

Bittersweet Chocolate Tarts

MAKES 10 TARTS

- ¾ cup whipping cream
- 1½ cups bittersweet chocolate chips *or* 8 ounces bittersweet chocolate, chopped
- 1½ cups graham cracker crumbs
- 6 tablespoons (¾ stick) butter, melted
- ⅓ cup sugar
- Sweetened whipped cream (optional)

1. Heat ¾ cup cream to a simmer in microwave or on stovetop. Place chocolate in medium bowl; pour hot cream over chocolate. Let stand 1 minute; stir until smooth. Set filling aside to thicken while preparing tart crusts.
2. Preheat oven to 350°F. Spray 10 (3-inch) nonstick tart pans with nonstick cooking spray or line 10 standard (2½-inch) muffin cups with paper baking cups.
3. Combine graham cracker crumbs, butter and sugar in medium bowl; mix well. Press 2½ tablespoons crumb mixture into each prepared tart pan. (If using muffin cups, press crumb mixture evenly onto bottoms and two thirds up sides of cups.)
4. Bake crusts about 8 minutes or until lightly browned. Cool completely on wire rack or refrigerate 15 minutes to speed up cooling.
5. To remove crusts from pans, invert tart pan onto plate, one at a time. Tap bottom of pan firmly with hand to release crust from pan. (If using muffin pans, remove paper baking cups from pans; peel off paper cups from crusts.) Spread 2 tablespoons chocolate filling in each crust. Serve with whipped cream, if desired.

Tip

To make sweetened whipped cream, beat ½ cup cold whipping cream and 2 tablespoons powdered sugar in small bowl with electric mixer at high speed about 1½ minutes or until stiff peaks form.

Chocolate Peanut Butter Pie

MAKES 8 SERVINGS

- 10 whole chocolate graham crackers, broken into pieces
- 2 tablespoons granulated sugar
- ¼ cup (½ stick) butter, melted
- 1 package (8 ounces) cream cheese, softened
- 1 cup creamy peanut butter
- 1¾ cups powdered sugar, divided
- 3 tablespoons butter, softened
- 1¾ teaspoons vanilla, divided
- ¼ teaspoon salt
- 2 cups cold whipping cream
- ½ cup unsweetened cocoa powder
- 2 packages (1½ ounces each) chocolate peanut butter cups, chopped

1. Preheat oven to 350°F. Combine graham crackers and granulated sugar in food processor; process until finely ground. Add ¼ cup melted butter; process until well blended. Press into bottom and up side of 9-inch pie plate.
2. Bake crust 8 minutes. Cool completely on wire rack.
3. Meanwhile, beat cream cheese, peanut butter, ¾ cup powdered sugar, 3 tablespoons softened butter, 1 teaspoon vanilla and salt in large bowl with electric mixer at medium speed about 3 minutes or until light and fluffy.
4. Spread filling in cooled crust; smooth top. Refrigerate pie while preparing topping.
5. Beat cream, cocoa, remaining 1 cup powdered sugar and ¾ teaspoon vanilla in medium bowl with electric mixer at high speed 1 to 2 minutes or until soft peaks form.
6. Spread chocolate whipped cream over peanut butter layer; sprinkle with peanut butter cups. Refrigerate several hours or overnight.

Chocolate Chess Pie

MAKES 8 SERVINGS

- **4 ounces unsweetened chocolate, chopped**
- **3 tablespoons butter**
- **3 eggs**
- **1 egg yolk**
- **1¼ cups sugar**
- **½ cup half-and-half**
- **1 to 2 teaspoons instant coffee granules**
- **¼ teaspoon salt**
- **1 unbaked 9-inch pie crust**
- **Whipped cream**
- **Chocolate-covered coffee beans (optional)**

1. Preheat oven to 325°F.
2. Combine chocolate and butter in small saucepan; heat over low heat until melted, stirring frequently. Set aside to cool 15 minutes.
3. Whisk eggs and egg yolk in medium bowl. Whisk in sugar, half-and-half, coffee granules and salt until well blended. Whisk in chocolate mixture until smooth. Pour into unbaked crust.
4. Bake 35 minutes or until set. Cool completely on wire rack. Refrigerate 2 hours or until ready to serve. Serve with whipped cream; garnish with chocolate-covered coffee beans.

Tip

Use 2 teaspoons instant coffee granules for a more pronounced coffee flavor; use a smaller amount if a more subtle coffee flavor is preferred.

Caramel Chocolate Tart

MAKES 8 SERVINGS

Crust

- ¾ cup all-purpose flour
- ¾ cup unsweetened cocoa powder
- ½ cup (1 stick) cold butter, cubed
- 3 tablespoons sugar
- ⅛ teaspoon salt
- 3 tablespoons whipping cream
- 1 egg
- 1 egg yolk

Filling

- 1 cup sugar
- ¼ cup water
- 2 tablespoons light corn syrup
- 5 tablespoons butter
- ¼ cup whipping cream
- 1 teaspoon vanilla

Ganache

- ½ cup plus 1 tablespoon whipping cream
- 4 ounces bittersweet chocolate, chopped
- Fresh raspberries (optional)

1. For crust, beat flour, cocoa, ½ cup cold butter, 3 tablespoons sugar and salt in large bowl with electric mixer at medium speed until mixture resembles coarse crumbs. Beat in 3 tablespoons cream, egg and egg yolk just until combined. Wrap dough in plastic wrap; refrigerate at least 1 hour or up to 3 days.
2. Roll out dough into 10-inch circle (about ¼ inch thick) on floured surface. Press into bottom and up side of 9-inch tart pan; trim edge even with edge of pan. Prick bottom with fork. Cover and refrigerate 30 minutes.
3. Preheat oven to 350°F. Line tart shell with foil and fill with pie weights or dried beans. Bake crust 15 minutes. Remove foil and pie weights; bake 10 to 12 minutes. Cool completely on wire rack.
4. For filling, combine 1 cup sugar, water and corn syrup in medium saucepan; cook and stir over medium-high heat until sugar is completely melted and deep amber color. Remove from heat; whisk in 5 tablespoons butter, ¼ cup cream and vanilla until blended. Let stand 5 minutes to cool slightly. Pour into cooled crust; let stand 45 minutes or until set.
5. For ganache, heat ½ cup plus 1 tablespoon cream to a simmer in microwave or on stovetop. Place chocolate in medium bowl. Whisk cream into chocolate until smooth and well blended.
6. Pour ganache over caramel filling, tilting pan to cover completely. Refrigerate 2 hours or until set. Garnish with raspberries.

Italian Chocolate Pie

MAKES 8 SERVINGS

- ¼ cup pine nuts
- 3 tablespoons packed brown sugar
- 1 tablespoon grated orange peel
- 1 unbaked 9-inch pie crust
- 4 ounces bittersweet chocolate, coarsely chopped
- 3 tablespoons butter
- 1 can (5 ounces) evaporated milk
- 3 eggs
- 3 tablespoons hazelnut liqueur
- 1 teaspoon vanilla
- Whipped cream (optional)
- Chocolate curls (optional)

1. Toast pine nuts in dry nonstick skillet over medium heat until golden brown, stirring constantly. Finely chop pine nuts; cool to room temperature.
2. Combine pine nuts, brown sugar and orange peel in small bowl; mix well. Sprinkle onto bottom of pie crust; press gently into crust.
3. Preheat oven to 325°F. Combine chocolate and butter in small saucepan; heat over low heat until melted, stirring frequently. Set aside to cool to room temperature.
4. Beat chocolate mixture and evaporated milk in medium bowl with electric mixer at medium speed until blended. Add eggs, one at a time, beating well after each addition. Stir in hazelnut liqueur and vanilla. Pour into crust.
5. Bake on center rack of oven 30 to 40 minutes or until set. Cool completely on wire rack. Refrigerate until ready to serve. Serve with whipped cream and chocolate curls, if desired.

White Chocolate Cranberry Tart

MAKES 8 SERVINGS

- 1 refrigerated pie crust (half of 14-ounce package)
- 1 cup sugar
- 2 eggs
- ¼ cup (½ stick) butter, melted
- 2 teaspoons vanilla
- ½ cup all-purpose flour
- 6 ounces white chocolate, chopped
- ½ cup chopped macadamia nuts, toasted*
- ½ cup dried cranberries, coarsely chopped
- Whipped cream, grated orange peel and white chocolate shavings (optional)

***To toast nuts, cook in small skillet over medium heat about 3 minutes or until fragrant, stirring frequently.**

1. Preheat oven to 350°F. Press crust into 9-inch tart pan with removable bottom or 9-inch pie plate.
2. Whisk sugar, eggs, butter and vanilla in large bowl until well blended. Stir in flour until blended. Add white chocolate, macadamia nuts and cranberries; mix well. Pour into unbaked crust.
3. Bake 50 to 55 minutes or until top of tart is golden brown and knife inserted into center comes out clean. Cool completely on wire rack. Garnish with whipped cream, orange peel and white chocolate shavings.

Fudgy Bittersweet Brownie Pie

MAKES 12 SERVINGS

- 12 ounces bittersweet chocolate*
- ½ cup (1 stick) butter
- 2 eggs
- ½ cup sugar
- 1 cup all-purpose flour
- ½ teaspoon salt
- ¾ cup hot fudge topping
- ¾ cup caramel ice cream topping
- ¾ cup chopped pecans

** Or substitute 4 ounces unsweetened chocolate plus 8 ounces semisweet chocolate, if desired.*

1. Preheat oven to 350°F. Spray 10-inch tart pan with removable bottom or 9-inch square baking pan with nonstick cooking spray.
2. Combine chocolate and butter in small saucepan; heat over low heat until melted, stirring frequently. Set aside to cool slightly.
3. Beat eggs in medium bowl with electric mixer at medium speed 30 seconds. Gradually add sugar; beat 1 minute. Beat in chocolate mixture, scraping down side of bowl once. Add flour and salt; beat at low speed just until blended, scraping down side of bowl once. Spread batter evenly in prepared pan.
4. Bake 25 minutes or until center is just set. Cool completely in pan on wire rack.
5. To serve, cut pie into wedges (or squares if using square pan). Heat hot fudge and caramel toppings according to package directions. Drizzle 1 tablespoon of each topping over each serving; sprinkle with pecans.

Raspberry Chocolate Mousse Pie

MAKES 10 SERVINGS

- **40** chocolate wafer cookies, finely crushed
- **½** cup (1 stick) butter, melted
- **½** cup water
- **7** tablespoons sugar
- **5** egg yolks
- **6** ounces semisweet chocolate, melted and cooled slightly
- **3** tablespoons raspberry-flavored liqueur (optional)
- **3½** cups thawed frozen whipped topping
- Whipped cream, fresh raspberries and fresh mint sprigs (optional)

1. Combine cookie crumbs and butter in medium bowl; mix well. Press into bottom of 9-inch springform pan.
2. Combine water and sugar in medium saucepan; bring to a boil over medium-high heat. Boil 1 minute.
3. Place egg yolks in large bowl. Gradually whisk in hot sugar mixture until well blended. Return mixture to medium saucepan; whisk over low heat 1 to 2 minutes or until mixture is thick and creamy. Remove from heat; pour mixture back into large bowl. Whisk in melted chocolate and liqueur, if desired. Beat mixture until cool. Fold in whipped topping until blended.
4. Pour mixture into prepared crust; freeze until firm. Let pie stand at room temperature 20 minutes before serving.
5. Remove side of pan; garnish with whipped cream, raspberries and mint.

Chocolate Walnut Toffee Tart

MAKES 12 SERVINGS

- 2 cups all-purpose flour
- 1¼ cups plus 3 tablespoons sugar, divided
- ¾ cup (1½ sticks) butter, cut into pieces
- 2 egg yolks
- 1¼ cups whipping cream
- 1 teaspoon ground cinnamon
- 2 teaspoons vanilla
- 2 cups coarsely chopped walnuts
- 1¼ cups semisweet chocolate chips or chunks, divided

1. Preheat oven to 325°F. Line baking sheet with foil.
2. Combine flour and 3 tablespoons sugar in food processor; pulse just until blended. Scatter butter over flour mixture; process 20 seconds. Add egg yolks; process 10 seconds (mixture may be crumbly).
3. Press dough firmly into ungreased 10-inch tart pan with removable bottom or 9- or 10-inch pie plate. Bake 10 minutes or until surface is no longer shiny. Place tart pan on prepared baking sheet. *Increase oven temperature to 375°F.*
4. Combine remaining 1¼ cups sugar, cream and cinnamon in medium saucepan; bring to a boil over medium-high heat. Reduce heat to medium-low; simmer 10 minutes, stirring frequently. Remove from heat; stir in vanilla. Sprinkle walnuts and 1 cup chocolate chips evenly over crust. Pour cream mixture over top.
5. Bake 35 to 40 minutes or until filling is bubbly and crust is lightly browned. Cool completely on wire rack.
6. Place remaining ¼ cup chocolate chips in small resealable food storage bag. Microwave on HIGH 20 seconds; knead bag until chocolate is melted. Cut small hole in one corner of bag; drizzle chocolate over tart.

Chocolate Caramel Surprise Pie

MAKES 10 SERVINGS

- 1½ cups plus 6 tablespoons whipping cream, divided
- 8 ounces semisweet chocolate, chopped, divided
- 1 (6-ounce) chocolate crumb pie crust
- ¼ cup caramel ice cream topping
- 6 tablespoons sugar, divided
- ¼ teaspoon salt
- 3 egg yolks
- ½ teaspoon vanilla
- Whipped topping and caramels (optional)

1. Combine ½ cup cream and 4 ounces chocolate in small heavy saucepan; heat over low heat until chocolate is melted and mixture is smooth, stirring frequently. Cool slightly. Spread evenly in crust. Refrigerate 30 minutes.
2. Spread caramel topping over chocolate layer. Refrigerate 30 minutes.
3. Combine 1 cup cream and remaining 4 ounces chocolate in same saucepan; heat over low heat until chocolate is melted and mixture is smooth, stirring frequently. Stir in 4 tablespoons sugar and salt; set aside to cool slightly.
4. Whisk egg yolks in small bowl. Pour ½ cup chocolate mixture into egg yolks, whisking constantly. Pour egg mixture back into saucepan; cook and stir over low heat until mixture is thickened. Cook 1 minute. (Mixture should reach 160°F.) Transfer to large bowl; stir in vanilla. Refrigerate 30 minutes, stirring occasionally.
5. Beat remaining 6 tablespoons cream and 2 tablespoons sugar in small bowl with electric mixer at high speed until stiff peaks form. Fold whipped cream into chocolate mixture until blended. Gently spread over caramel layer. Refrigerate 4 hours or overnight. Garnish with whipped topping and caramels.

Decadent Desserts

Frozen Hot Chocolate Pops

MAKES 6 POPS

- 1 cup milk
- 2 ounces semisweet chocolate, finely chopped
- 3 tablespoons sugar
- 2 tablespoons hot chocolate mix
- 2 cups chocolate ice cream
- Pop molds or paper or plastic cups
- Pop sticks

1. Combine milk, chopped chocolate, sugar and hot chocolate mix in small microwavable bowl; microwave on HIGH 30 seconds. Stir; microwave at 30-second intervals until chocolate is melted and mixture is smooth, stirring after each interval. Cool to room temperature, about 1 hour.
2. Pour chocolate mixture into blender or food processor; add ice cream and blend until smooth.
3. Pour mixture into molds. Cover top of each mold with small piece of foil. Freeze 2 hours.*
4. Insert sticks through center of foil. Freeze 4 to 6 hours or until firm.
5. To remove pops from molds, remove foil and place bottoms of pops under warm running water until loosened. Press firmly on bottoms to release. (Do not twist or pull sticks.)

**If using pop molds with lids, skip step 4 and freeze until firm.*

Double Chocolate Cookies and Cream Mousse

MAKES 8 SERVINGS

- **8 ounces semisweet chocolate, chopped**
- **2½ cups chilled whipping cream, divided**
- **4 egg yolks**
- **Pinch of salt**
- **1¼ teaspoons vanilla, divided**
- **¼ cup granulated sugar**
- **23 chocolate sandwich cookies, divided**
- **1 tablespoon powdered sugar**

1. Melt chocolate in medium saucepan over very low heat, stirring frequently. Remove from heat; stir in ¼ cup cream until well blended.
2. Combine egg yolks and salt in medium bowl. Whisk about half of chocolate mixture into egg yolks until blended; whisk egg yolk mixture back into chocolate mixture in saucepan. Cook over low heat 2 minutes, whisking constantly. Remove from heat; cool to room temperature.
3. Beat 1¾ cups cream and 1 teaspoon vanilla in large bowl with electric mixer at high speed until soft peaks form. Gradually beat in granulated sugar; beat until stiff peaks form. Fold about one fourth of whipped cream into chocolate mixture; fold chocolate mixture into remaining whipped cream until blended.
4. Finely chop two cookies; fold into mousse. Coarsely chop two cookies for topping. Cut remaining 19 cookies into quarters; set aside. Refrigerate mousse 4 hours or overnight.
5. Beat remaining ½ cup cream in medium bowl with electric mixer at high speed 30 seconds or until thickened. Add powdered sugar and remaining ¼ teaspoon vanilla; beat until stiff peaks form.
6. Spoon ¼ cup mousse into each of eight wide-mouth half-pint jars. Top with ¼ cup quartered cookies and another ¼ cup mousse. Garnish with dollop of sweetened whipped cream and chopped cookies.

Ice Cream Pizza Treat

MAKES 8 SERVINGS

- **24 chocolate sandwich cookies**
- **1 jar (about 12 ounces) hot fudge ice cream topping, divided**
- **2 pints vanilla ice cream**
- **⅓ cup candy-coated chocolate pieces**

1. Place cookies in food processor; pulse until large crumbs form. (Do not overprocess into fine crumbs.)
2. Add ½ cup hot fudge topping; pulse just until blended. (Mixture should not be smooth; small cookie pieces may remain.)
3. Transfer mixture to pizza pan; press into 11- to 12-inch circle about ¼ inch thick. Freeze crust 10 minutes. Meanwhile, remove ice cream from freezer to soften 10 minutes.
4. Spread ice cream evenly over crust (about ½-inch-thick layer), leaving ½-inch border. Return to freezer; freeze 2 hours or until firm.
5. Heat remaining hot fudge topping according to package directions. Drizzle over ice cream; top with chocolate pieces. Freeze 1 hour or until firm. Cut into wedges to serve.

Chocolate Chip Cookie Delights

MAKES 18 SERVINGS

- 1¾ cups all-purpose flour
- ¾ teaspoon salt
- ¾ teaspoon baking powder
- ½ teaspoon baking soda
- 10 tablespoons (1¼ sticks) butter, softened
- ½ cup plus 2 tablespoons packed brown sugar
- ½ cup granulated sugar
- 1 egg
- 1 teaspoon vanilla
- 1½ cups semisweet or bittersweet chocolate chips
- Flaky sea salt (optional)
- Vanilla ice cream (optional)

1. Preheat oven to 375°F. Spray 18 standard (2½-inch) muffin cups with nonstick cooking spray.

2. Combine flour, ¾ teaspoon salt, baking powder and baking soda in small bowl; mix well. Beat butter, brown sugar and granulated sugar in large bowl with electric mixer at medium-high speed about 5 minutes or until very light and fluffy. Add egg; beat until blended. Beat in vanilla. Stir in flour mixture until blended. Stir in chocolate chips.

3. Spoon scant ¼ cup dough into each prepared muffin cup; sprinkle with sea salt, if desired.

4. Bake about 14 minutes or until edges are golden brown but centers are still soft. Cool in pans 5 minutes; invert onto wire racks. Turn right side up; serve warm with ice cream, if desired.

Chocolate-Covered Cheesecake Pops

MAKES 24 POPS

- 1 package (8 ounces) cream cheese, softened
- ⅓ cup sugar
- 1 teaspoon vanilla
- 1 cup whipping cream, chilled
- ¼ cup mini semisweet chocolate chips
- Pop sticks
- 1 pound semisweet chocolate, chopped
- Multi-colored sprinkles

1. Beat cream cheese, sugar and vanilla in medium bowl with electric mixer at medium-high speed about 2 minutes or until well blended and smooth.
2. Beat cream in large bowl with electric mixer at high speed until stiff peaks form. Gradually beat in cream cheese mixture, scraping down side of bowl after each addition. Stir in chocolate chips. Cover and refrigerate 2 hours or until firm.
3. Line baking sheet with parchment paper. Gently roll cheesecake mixture into 24 balls; place on prepared baking sheet. Freeze 1 hour.
4. Insert sticks into cheesecake balls; freeze 2 hours or until firm.
5. Melt chocolate in top of double boiler over simmering water, stirring occasionally. Working with one at a time, dip frozen cheesecake balls in chocolate, rotating to coat evenly and letting excess chocolate drip off. Top with sprinkles.
6. Return cheesecake pops to baking sheet; freeze 1 hour or until firm.

Chocolate Peanut Crunch

MAKES ABOUT ¾ POUND

- **1 cup milk chocolate chips**
- **½ cup semisweet chocolate chips**
- **2 tablespoons corn syrup**
- **1 tablespoon shortening**
- **½ cup roasted peanuts**
- **2 teaspoons vanilla**

1. Spray 8-inch square baking pan with nonstick cooking spray.
2. Melt milk chocolate and semisweet chocolate chips, corn syrup and shortening in small saucepan over low heat, stirring constantly.
3. Stir in peanuts and vanilla. Spread in prepared pan, distributing peanuts evenly. Refrigerate until firm. Break into pieces.

Intense Chocolate Ice Cream

MAKES 4 SERVINGS

- **2 cups plain rice milk, divided**
- **¼ cup tapioca flour**
- **¼ cup unsweetened cocoa powder**
- **6 tablespoons sugar**
- **¼ teaspoon salt**
- **⅓ cup semisweet chocolate chips**
- **½ teaspoon vanilla**
- **Fresh berries (optional)**

1. Whisk ½ cup rice milk, tapioca flour and cocoa in medium saucepan until smooth. Whisk in remaining 1½ cups rice milk. Whisk in sugar and salt until well blended. Cook over medium heat until mixture thickens to consistency of pudding, whisking constantly.
2. Remove from heat; stir in chocolate chips and vanilla until chocolate is melted and mixture is smooth. Transfer to medium bowl; cover and refrigerate 2 hours or until cold.
3. Pour into ice cream maker; process according to manufacturer's directions. Serve with berries, if desired.

Fudgy Marshmallow Popcorn

MAKES ABOUT 4 QUARTS

- 3½ quarts popped popcorn (about 14 cups)
- 2 cups sugar
- 1 cup evaporated milk
- ¼ cup (½ stick) butter
- 1 cup marshmallow creme (half of 7-ounce jar)
- 1 cup semisweet chocolate chips
- 1 teaspoon vanilla

1. Line baking sheets with with parchment paper or spray with nonstick cooking spray. Place popcorn in large bowl.
2. Combine sugar, evaporated milk and butter in medium saucepan; cook over medium heat until sugar is dissolved and mixture comes to a boil, stirring constantly.* Boil 5 minutes.
3. Remove from heat; stir in marshmallow creme, chocolate chips and vanilla until chocolate is melted and mixture is smooth.
4. Pour chocolate mixture over popcorn, stirring until completely coated. Spread in single layer on prepared baking sheets. Refrigerate until set.

**If sugar mixture sticks to the pan, wash down side of pan with pastry brush frequently dipped in hot water to remove crystals.*

Tip

Remove any unpopped kernels before measuring the popped popcorn.

Black Forest Cobbler

MAKES 8 TO 10 SERVINGS

Filling

- **3 pounds frozen pitted sweet cherries, thawed and drained**
- **¾ cup sugar**
- **¼ cup cornstarch**
- **2 tablespoons lemon juice**
- **1 teaspoon vanilla**

Biscuit Topping

- **1¼ cups all-purpose flour**
- **½ cup sugar**
- **¼ cup unsweetened cocoa powder**
- **1½ teaspoons baking powder**
- **1 teaspoon baking soda**
- **½ teaspoon salt**
- **6 tablespoons (¾ stick) cold butter, cut into small pieces**
- **½ cup semisweet chocolate chips**
- **⅔ cup buttermilk**

1. Preheat oven to 375°F. Spray 9-inch square baking dish with nonstick cooking spray.
2. For filling, combine cherries, ¾ cup sugar, cornstarch, lemon juice and vanilla in large bowl; stir to coat. Spoon into prepared baking dish.
3. For topping, combine flour, ½ cup sugar, cocoa, baking powder, baking soda and salt in medium bowl; mix well. Cut in butter with pastry blender or mix with fingertips until mixture resembles coarse crumbs. Stir in chocolate chips. Add buttermilk; stir just until combined. *Do not overmix.*
4. Drop topping, 2 tablespoonfuls at a time, into mounds over cherry mixture.
5. Bake 40 to 45 minutes or until filling is bubbly and toothpick inserted into center of topping comes out clean. Let stand 30 minutes before serving. Serve warm.

Chocolate Bourbon Bites

MAKES 6 DOZEN MINI CUPCAKES

Cupcakes

- 1 package (about 15 ounces) devil's food cake mix
- 1 cup buttermilk*
- 3 eggs
- ⅓ cup bourbon
- ¼ cup (½ stick) butter, melted and cooled
- 1 cup mini semisweet chocolate chips

Frosting

- 3 cups powdered sugar
- 1 cup unsweetened cocoa powder
- ½ cup (1 stick) butter, softened
- ⅓ cup milk
- ¼ cup bourbon
- 1 teaspoon vanilla

**Or substitute 1 tablespoon vinegar or lemon juice plus enough milk to equal 1 cup. Stir; let stand 5 minutes.*

1. For cupcakes, preheat oven to 350°F. Line 72 mini (1¾-inch) muffin cups with paper baking cups or place 72 mini foil baking cups on baking sheets.
2. Beat cake mix, buttermilk, eggs, ⅓ cup bourbon and ¼ cup melted butter in large bowl with electric mixer at low speed 30 seconds. Beat at medium speed 2 minutes. Stir in chocolate chips. Spoon batter evenly into prepared muffin cups.
3. Bake 10 to 12 minutes or until toothpick inserted into centers comes out clean. Cool in pans 5 minutes; remove to wire racks to cool completely.
4. For frosting, beat powdered sugar, cocoa, ½ cup softened butter, milk, ¼ cup bourbon and vanilla in large bowl with electric mixer at medium speed until smooth. Frost cupcakes.

Tip

If you don't have enough mini muffin pans or oven space to bake all the mini cupcakes at once, bake them in batches. Let the extra batter stand at room temperature while each batch bakes.

Chocolate Crème Brûlée

MAKES 4 SERVINGS

- **2 cups whipping cream**
- **3 ounces semisweet or bittersweet baking chocolate, finely chopped**
- **3 egg yolks**
- **¼ cup granulated sugar**
- **2 teaspoons vanilla**
- **3 tablespoons packed brown sugar**

1. Preheat oven to 325°F. Heat cream in medium saucepan over medium heat until it begins to simmer. *Do not boil.* Remove from heat; stir in chocolate until melted and smooth. Set aside to cool slightly.
2. Beat egg yolks and granulated sugar in large bowl with electric mixer at medium-high speed 5 minutes or until thick and pale yellow. Beat in chocolate mixture and vanilla until blended.
3. Divide mixture among four 6-ounce shallow baking dishes or custard cups. Place dishes in baking pan; place pan in oven. Pour boiling water into baking pan to reach halfway up sides of baking dishes. Cover pan loosely with foil.
4. Bake 30 minutes or just until edges are set. Remove baking dishes to wire rack to cool completely. Cover with plastic wrap; refrigerate 4 hours or up to 3 days.
5. When ready to serve, preheat broiler. Spread about 2 teaspoons brown sugar evenly over each cup. Broil 3 to 4 minutes or until sugar bubbles and browns. Serve immediately.

Triple Chocolate Pops

MAKES 3 POPS

- 1 cup chocolate ice cream
- ¼ cup milk
- 1 tablespoon chocolate syrup
- ½ cup crushed chocolate wafers
- 3 (5-ounce) plastic or paper cups or pop molds
- 3 pop sticks
- 6 tablespoons quick-hardening chocolate shell dessert topping

1. Combine ice cream, milk and chocolate syrup in blender or food processor; blend until smooth. Add crushed wafers; pulse just until combined.
2. Pour mixture into cups, filling two-thirds full. Freeze 1 hour.
3. Insert sticks. Spoon 2 tablespoons chocolate shell topping into each cup over ice cream layer. *Do not cover.* Freeze 4 to 6 hours or until firm.
4. To serve, gently twist frozen pops out of plastic cups or peel away paper cups.

Chocolate Hazelnut Mousse

MAKES 8 SERVINGS

- **1 package (4-serving size) chocolate instant pudding and pie filling mix**
- **2 cups milk**
- **½ cup chocolate hazelnut spread**
- **1½ cups thawed frozen whipped topping, plus additional for garnish (optional)**
- **Fresh strawberries, halved (optional)**

1. Prepare pudding with milk in medium bowl according to package directions. Whisk in chocolate hazelnut spread until well blended. Refrigerate 15 minutes.
2. Gently fold 1½ cups whipped topping into pudding.
3. Spoon mixture into dessert dishes, ramekins or small bowls. Refrigerate until ready to serve. Garnish with additional whipped topping and strawberries.

Rich Chocolate Pudding

MAKES 4 SERVINGS

- ⅔ cup sugar
- ¼ cup unsweetened cocoa powder
- 3 tablespoons cornstarch
- 2 cups milk
- 1 egg
- 1 tablespoon butter
- ½ teaspoon vanilla

1. Combine sugar, cocoa and cornstarch in medium saucepan; whisk in milk until well blended. Cook over medium-high heat until mixture boils, whisking frequently. Boil 1 minute, whisking constantly.
2. Beat egg in small bowl. Whisk about ½ cup hot milk mixture into egg; whisk egg mixture back into saucepan. Cook over medium heat 2 minutes, whisking constantly.
3. Remove pudding from heat; stir in butter and vanilla until blended. Pour into four individual serving dishes. Serve warm or cover and refrigerate until ready to serve.

Rich Mocha Pudding

Add 1 to 1½ teaspoons instant coffee granules to sugar mixture in step 1.

Drinkable Chocolate

Cookies and Cream Shake

MAKES 1 SERVING

- **5 chocolate sandwich cookies, divided**
- **¼ cup whole milk**
- **2 cups vanilla ice cream**
- **Whipped cream or whipped topping**

1. Coarsely chop four cookies. Finely chop remaining cookie; set aside for garnish.
2. Pour milk into blender; add ice cream and blend until smooth. Add coarsely chopped cookies; pulse until blended.
3. Top shake with whipped cream; sprinkle with reserved chopped cookies.

Peppermint Hot Chocolate

MAKES 2 SERVINGS

- ¼ cup water
- 3 tablespoons sugar
- 2 tablespoons unsweetened Dutch process cocoa powder
- Pinch of salt
- 1¼ cups milk
- ½ teaspoon vanilla
- ½ teaspoon peppermint extract
- Whipped cream
- Mini chocolate chips

1. Combine water, sugar, cocoa and salt in small saucepan; whisk until blended. Bring to a simmer over medium-high heat, whisking frequently.
2. Stir in milk and vanilla; cook until steaming, whisking frequently. *Do not boil.* Stir in peppermint extract.
3. Pour into mugs; top with whipped cream and chocolate chips.

Chocolate Frosty

MAKES 2 TO 3 SERVINGS

- 2 cups milk, divided
- ¼ cup unsweetened cocoa powder
- ½ cup sweetened condensed milk
- 1 tablespoon corn syrup
- 1 teaspoon vanilla

1. Whisk ¼ cup milk and cocoa in large measuring cup with pour spout until well blended. Whisk in 1½ cups milk, sweetened condensed milk, corn syrup and vanilla. Pour mixture into ice cube tray. Freeze 4 hours or until firm.
2. Loosen frozen chocolate cubes with thin knife; remove from ice cube trays. Place in blender with remaining ¼ cup milk; pulse to break up chunks. Blend about 30 seconds or until smooth.

Chocolate Cake Milkshake

MAKES 1 SERVING

- **1 slice (⅛ of cake) Rich Chocolate Cake (recipe follows)**
- **½ cup milk**
- **2 scoops vanilla ice cream (about 1 cup total)**

1. Prepare and frost Rich Chocolate Cake.
2. Combine milk, ice cream and cake slice in blender; blend just until cake is incorporated but texture of shake is not completely smooth.

Rich Chocolate Cake

MAKES 8 TO 10 SERVINGS

- **1 package (about 15 ounces) devil's food cake mix**
- **1 cup cold water**
- **1 cup mayonnaise**
- **3 eggs**
- **1½ containers (16 ounces each) chocolate frosting**

1. Preheat oven to 350°F. Spray two 9-inch round cake pans with nonstick cooking spray.
2. Beat cake mix, water, mayonnaise and eggs in large bowl with electric mixer at low speed 30 seconds. Beat at medium speed 2 minutes. Pour batter into prepared pans.
3. Bake 25 minutes or until toothpick inserted into centers comes out clean. Cool in pans 10 minutes; remove to wire racks to cool completely.
4. Fill and frost cake with chocolate frosting.

"Hot" Chocolate Smoothie

MAKES 4 SERVINGS

- 2½ cups chocolate frozen yogurt or ice cream
- 1¾ cups chocolate milk
- 1 banana
- ⅛ teaspoon chipotle chili powder
- 1½ cups cubed or crushed ice
- Whipped cream and chocolate shavings (optional)

1. Combine frozen yogurt, milk, banana, chili powder and ice in blender; blend until smooth.
2. Pour into glasses; garnish with whipped cream and chocolate shavings.

Peanut Butter Hot Chocolate

MAKES 2 SERVINGS

- 2 cups milk
- ½ cup semisweet or milk chocolate chips or chopped chocolate
- 2 tablespoons creamy peanut butter

1. Combine milk, chocolate chips and peanut butter in small saucepan or microwavable measuring cup; bring to a simmer over medium heat, stirring frequently.
2. Reduce heat to low; cook and stir 1 minute or until well blended and smooth.

Viennese Coffee

MAKES ABOUT 4 SERVINGS

- 1 cup whipping cream, divided
- 1 teaspoon powdered sugar
- 3 ounces bittersweet or semisweet chocolate, chopped
- 3 cups strong freshly brewed hot coffee
- ¼ cup crème de cacao or Irish cream (optional)
- Chocolate shavings (optional)

1. Combine ⅔ cup cream and powdered sugar in chilled medium bowl; beat with electric mixer at high speed until soft peaks form. Cover and refrigerate until ready to serve.
2. Heat remaining ⅓ cup cream to a simmer in small saucepan over medium-low heat. Stir in chocolate. Remove from heat; cover and let stand 5 minutes or until chocolate is melted. Stir until smooth.
3. Add hot coffee to chocolate mixture; heat over low heat just until bubbles form around edge of pan and coffee is heated through, stirring frequently. Remove from heat; stir in crème de cacao, if desired.
4. Pour into warmed mugs. Top with whipped cream; garnish with chocolate shavings.

Frozen Hot Chocolate

MAKES 3 TO 4 SERVINGS

- ½ cup milk
- 3 tablespoons sugar
- 3 ounces finely chopped semisweet chocolate *or* ⅔ cup semisweet chocolate chips
- 1 tablespoon hot chocolate mix powder
- 4 scoops chocolate ice cream
- 2 cups ice cubes
- Whipped cream, chocolate sprinkles or mini marshmallows (optional)

1. Combine milk, sugar, chopped chocolate and hot chocolate mix in medium microwavable bowl; microwave on HIGH 30 seconds. Stir until chocolate is melted and mixture is smooth. Cool to room temperature, about 1 hour (or refrigerate and bring to room temperature when ready to serve).
2. Combine chocolate mixture, ice cream and ice in blender; blend until smooth.
3. Pour into glasses; garnish with whipped cream and sprinkles. Serve immediately.

Coconut Cream Pie Chiller

MAKES 4 SERVINGS

- 1½ cups vanilla frozen yogurt
- 1½ cups chocolate frozen yogurt
- ¾ cup light coconut milk
- ½ cup sweetened flaked coconut, divided
- 2 tablespoons cream of coconut
- 4 pineapple wedges (optional)

1. Combine vanilla and chocolate frozen yogurt, coconut milk, ¼ cup coconut and cream of coconut in blender; blend until smooth and creamy.
2. Pour into glasses; garnish with pineapple wedge, if desired. Sprinkle with remaining ¼ cup coconut. Serve immediately.

R

S

T

U

V

W

Metric Conversion Chart

VOLUME MEASUREMENTS (dry)

1/8 teaspoon = 0.5 mL
1/4 teaspoon = 1 mL
1/2 teaspoon = 2 mL
3/4 teaspoon = 4 mL
1 teaspoon = 5 mL
1 tablespoon = 15 mL
2 tablespoons = 30 mL
1/4 cup = 60 mL
1/3 cup = 75 mL
1/2 cup = 125 mL
2/3 cup = 150 mL
3/4 cup = 175 mL
1 cup = 250 mL
2 cups = 1 pint = 500 mL
3 cups = 750 mL
4 cups = 1 quart = 1 L

VOLUME MEASUREMENTS (fluid)

1 fluid ounce (2 tablespoons) = 30 mL
4 fluid ounces (1/2 cup) = 125 mL
8 fluid ounces (1 cup) = 250 mL
12 fluid ounces (1 1/2 cups) = 375 mL
16 fluid ounces (2 cups) = 500 mL

WEIGHTS (mass)

1/2 ounce = 15 g
1 ounce = 30 g
3 ounces = 90 g
4 ounces = 120 g
8 ounces = 225 g
10 ounces = 285 g
12 ounces = 360 g
16 ounces = 1 pound = 450 g

DIMENSIONS

1/16 inch = 2 mm
1/8 inch = 3 mm
1/4 inch = 6 mm
1/2 inch = 1.5 cm
3/4 inch = 2 cm
1 inch = 2.5 cm

OVEN TEMPERATURES

250°F = 120°C
275°F = 140°C
300°F = 150°C
325°F = 160°C
350°F = 180°C
375°F = 190°C
400°F = 200°C
425°F = 220°C
450°F = 230°C

BAKING PAN SIZES

Utensil	Size in Inches/Quarts	Metric Volume	Size in Centimeters
Baking or Cake Pan (square or rectangular)	8×8×2	2 L	20×20×5
	9×9×2	2.5 L	23×23×5
	12×8×2	3 L	30×20×5
	13×9×2	3.5 L	33×23×5
Loaf Pan	8×4×3	1.5 L	20×10×7
	9×5×3	2 L	23×13×7
Round Layer Cake Pan	8×1½	1.2 L	20×4
	9×1½	1.5 L	23×4
Pie Plate	8×1¼	750 mL	20×3
	9×1¼	1 L	23×3
Baking Dish or Casserole	1 quart	1 L	—
	1½ quart	1.5 L	—
	2 quart	2 L	—